Problems of sociology in education

Problems of sociology in education

Roger Girod

Prepared for the
International Bureau
of Education

Jessica Kingsley Publishers/Unesco

Jessica Kingsley Publishers ISBN 1 85302 031 1
Unesco ISBN 92-3-102582-1

First published in 1990 by Jessica Kingsley Publishers,
118 Pentonville Road, London N1 9JN
and
The United Nations Educational,
Scientific and Cultural Organization,
7, place de Fontenoy, 75700 Paris, France

British Library Cataloguing in Publication Data
Girod, Roger
    Problems of sociology in education. - (Educational
    sciences).
    1. Education. Social aspects
    I. Title II. Series
    370.19

    ISBN 1-85302-031-1

Printed and bound in Great Britain by
Biddles Ltd, Guildford and King's Lynn

Contents

Preface

It was in 1981 that the International Bureau of Education launched its the 'Educational sciences' series, a collection of monographs drawing their inspiration from the application of various sciences to education. *Empirical research in education, Cultural anthropology and education, The history of education today* are works in this series which, by their titles alone, recall the relationship between a science (understood as the scientific method) or sciences (meaning any rigorous discipline) and education. Indeed, all disciplines, inasmuch as they tackle the issues and circumstances of education in their historical, social, economic, technical and political contexts, could be covered by this series.

This monograph, the work of Roger Girod, a professor at the University of Geneva, follows in this tradition and reviews some of the principle problems of sociology in education:

- trends in the real level of education in modern societies;
- inequality of opportunity - particularly according to social origin - in the distribution of knowledge (real level of education), of qualifications (formal level of education) and social background.

The author has based this work on documentation originating from various countries. Some chapters serve as a useful introduction to the methods which play an important role in the analysis of situations affecting inequality of opportunity.

We express our warm thanks to Professor Girod who has contributed the fruit of his considerable labour to our series. As in the past, we remind readers that the ideas and opinions expressed in this work are those of the author and do not necessarily represent the views of Unesco. Furthermore, the designations employed and the presentation of the material throughout this publication do not imply the expression of any opinion whatsoever on the part of Unesco concerning the legal status of any country, territory, city or area or of its authorities, or concerning the delimitations of its frontiers or boundaries.

Introduction

This brief work examines some of the main *problems* arising in the sociology of education. It also attempts to shed light on the *methods* which are frequently employed in dealing with certain aspects of these problems and which may be unfamiliar to some of the readers for whom this book is intended.

The problems relate to two aspects of the level of education which, by virtue of schooling and all other factors involved, the population has attained.

The first of these aspects, the only one which statistical data and even many studies in the educational sciences normally take into account, is the level of education in the ordinary sense of the word. This aspect will be referred to in the present work as the formal level of education. On the basis of the formal level, we can break the population down into categories according to the highest level attained in the education system. For example: some primary school; complete primary studies; secondary-level studies; secondary school-leaving diploma (type A, type B, type C, etc.). The formal level of education tells us something, more or less accurately, depending on the specific mode of classification chosen about the duration and nature of schooling, as well as the kind of diploma obtained.

The other aspect of the level of education which we will concern ourselves with is the real level of education, that is, the level of knowledge individuals actually possess.

Data about the real level of education are very scarce, at least data which enable us to make the kinds of observations to which we will confine ourselves here. These observations must provide a composite picture of the outcome of society's educational efforts. Ideally, they would apply to the total population. In practice, however, we will have to content ourselves with data involving only certain age groups. But our observations will, nonetheless, be valid on the scale of entire generations, specifically generations of young adults.

Formal level and real level of education are far from going hand-in-hand. As we will point out, the former cannot be used as a satisfactory indicator of the latter and their evolution does not coincide.

We will also discuss the occupational situations to which various levels of formal education lead and the evolution of the relationship between the two. The latter point concerns the question of the evolution of the value of diplomas on the labour market.

In the pages which follow, we will also examine the problem of the inequality of opportunity. Such inequality is the result of the influence of circumstances over which the individual has absolutely no control - sex or social class, for example, - and which affect what life offers him/her. This problem is envisaged here from the point of view of access to education (in its real and formal aspects) and the distribution of occupations.

It is to this problem, namely, the inequality of opportunity, that the *methods* described relate. These methods consist of techniques for differentiating between the effects of the factors which account for differences. We will see how these techniques are applied: (a) in estimating the fraction attributable to the social background component and that attributable to the formal level of education (or, in the case of young pupils, of the kind of school attended) in the explanation of the inequality of real levels of education; and (b) in estimating the shares of these same factors in the explanation of the distribution of occupations.

                                                                    R. G.

CHAPTER ONE

Modernization of society and the evolution of the population's real level of general education

The subject of this and the chapter which follows should occupy the forefront of the educational sciences. Yet, for a long time, the educational sciences have entirely ignored them, at least when it comes to making genuine observations, rather than merely paying lip-service to them.

The topic thus ignored is that of the population's effective level of skills and knowledge. The intellectual level defined as such ought to be viewed from a great number of aspects, in particular the more elevated forms of literary education and scientific knowledge, or professional qualifications, etc.

Here, when speaking of general education, we will limit ourselves to more modest kinds of knowledge, most of which are taught in many schools (computer science, a second national language, for example), if not all of them (reading, etc.).

It might be observed that data and analyses on this subject abound. Are not pupils constantly being graded? Countless observations have been made on the results of educational experiments. But these do not provide us with the indications we need. Grading in school is generally done according to non-explicit criteria, which vary according to the person administering the test. It is thus difficult to assume, for example, that a country's degree of achievement at a given level of schooling is a reliable measurement of levels of knowledge. The experiments involve selected groups, often several grade levels, but rarely large numbers of individuals.

In any case, our investigation does not deal with children, but with *the real level of education which society has enabled its adult members to attain*. The time spent in school is only one phase in the process leading to this goal.

The primary objective of education in general, like that of education in particular, is, as a rule, to improve the skills of individuals, the effects of which should benefit them for the rest of their lives.

In this chapter we will simply report - which in itself is not, as we shall see, an easy task - on several aspects of the resultant combined action of all the factors involved. Some are related to education and all the others to, let us say, life in its biological, psychological and social - non-educational - aspects: the influence of standard of living, of family relationships, forms of production and trade, means of communication, etc.

The chapter which follows will examine the share of responsibility borne by education and by other factors, in particular, differences of social background.

Unfortunately, the documentation on the theme of the present chapter is still very meagre. Our files only contain a handful of evidence, even if we extend the scope of observation to adolescents 17 to 19 years old. Yet, with the help of researcher, to whom we owe a great debt of gratitude, we had access to some of the best data banks, in particular, those of Unesco and the Education Resources Information Center (ERIC). The indications needed should give a picture of the state of knowledge for entire generations, if not for the entire adult population. Indications of this type which we were able to find are confined essentially to the United States and Switzerland.

Trends

More complete data than that which we possess would no doubt reveal a great diversity of types of evolution, depending on the period, country, subject and criteria involved.

A fragment of the period of great progress in the real level of general education (Switzerland, late nineteenth and early twentieth centuries)

The kind of evolution generally expected is an elevation of the real level of knowledge, considered here as roughly parallel to the level of education in the sense of existing statistical data (the highest point reached in the education system).

We will refer to the statistical level of education as the *formal* level of education. This refers to the level which has theoretically been reached, in terms of diplomas, number of years of study, the level and type of schooling last undergone. The real level of education is the actual level of knowledge.

Formerly, in Switzerland, the two levels - formal and real - did, indeed, rise in parallel. The data which follow correspond to a rather lengthy segment of this phase which certainly began well before the period in question. It probably continued for a time thereafter. Further on, we will see that the trend was ultimately reversed.

In Switzerland, every year from 1875 to 1913, young men (usually at age 19) had to take a so-called 'pedagogical test' upon recruitment into the army. All Swiss males were involved. The exam was therefore administered to all male adolescents, including those recruits who would eventually be declared unfit for military service.

The pedagogical exam lasted for about two hours. The exercises it contained were of the primary education level. The purpose of the test was to obtain data in support of improvement efforts already under way in various regions of the country.

The test included the following subjects: reading (text comprehension); composition, arithmetic, civics (Swiss history and geography, its political institutions). The objective was not to evaluate how well the content of primary schooling had been memorized, but to examine to what extent young people around 20 years old, when confronted with problems and questions which adults must face, demonstrated that they possessed the abilities which the primary school had striven to instill in them since childhood.

Each year's exercise was chosen so as to maintain as constant a level as possible over time and uniformity between the various regions. The ranking of those questioned, by levels of ability, was carried out using very simple, explicitly formulated criteria.

Pierre Bovet, who criticized these national tests as having for many years placed an excessively heavy burden on teachers, nonetheless emphasized their high quality. He pointed out, fifteen years before Cattell began to popularize the idea of tests, that these exams constituted a kind of 'test' which was 'almost technically perfect', but which did not go by that name (Bovet, 1935, p. 36 & 199).

After several years of fine-tuning, the table for classifying those tested was set in 1879 and was not changed thereafter. It is therefore possible to trace the evolution quite closely from that date until the tests were done away with in 1913. This thirty-five year period was characterized by tremendous progress. On the eve of the First World War, the young men in

Table 1. General education: past trends. Example: young men, 19 years old for the most part. Switzerland: 1879–1913[1]

	I reading comprehension		II composition		III arithmetic		IV civics (history, geography pol. institutions)		I–IV average	
	1879	1913	1879	1913	1879	1913	1879	1913	1879	1913
The country as a whole										
1. good	34.0	63.5	24.9	42.2	28.9	49.4	19.7	33.3	26.9	47.1
2. acceptable	32.5	27.0	22.9	34.7	25.8	28.2	16.5	32.4	24.4	30.6
satisfactory (1+2)	66.5	90.5	47.8	76.9	54.7	77.6	36.2	65.7	51.3	77.7
3. unsatisfactory	33.5	9.5	52.2	23.1	45.3	22.4	63.8	34.3	48.7	23.3
Total (%)	100.0	100.0	100.0	100.0	100.0	100.0	100.0	100.0	100.0	100.0
Most advanced cantons [2]										
1. good	52.1	86.2	55.4	54.3	55.4	61.2	38.9	44.9	50.4	61.6
2. acceptable	32.9	12.2	20.6	33.4	23.6	28.9	26.0	35.8	25.8	27.6
satisfactory (1+2)	85.0	98.4	76.0	87.7	79.0	90.1	64.9	80.7	76.2	89.2
3. unsatisfactory	15.0	1.6	24.0	12.3	21.0	9.9	35.1	19.3	23.8	10.8
Total (%)	100.0	100.0	100.0	100.0	100.0	100.0	100.0	100.0	100.0	100.0
Least advanced cantons [3]										
1. good	11.4	50.0	4.5	33.5	4.9	35.6	4.1	31.1	6.2	37.6
2. acceptable	22.8	29.4	12.0	30.9	18.9	29.9	7.4	22.7	15.3	28.2
satisfactory (1+2)	34.2	79.4	16.5	64.4	23.8	65.5	11.5	53.8	21.5	65.8
3. unsatisfactory	65.8	20.6	83.5	35.6	76.2	34.5	88.5	46.2	78.5	34.2
Total (%)	100.0	100.0	100.0	100.0	100.0	100.0	100.0	100.0	100.0	100.0

1. *Pedagogical examination of 1880 recruits* (tested 1879) and *Pedagogical examination of recruits of the autumn of 1913*. Volumes 47 and 192 of 'Statistique de la Suisse'. Office of Statistics of the Federal Department of the Interior, Bern, 1880 and 1914. 1879 is the first year that the grading scheme, which was maintained until 1913, was implemented. Grades given by the examiners of the period: 1. *Good*. The level desired (the skills primary education strives to develop). 2. *Acceptable*. Other satisfactory scores. 3–5. *Unsatisfactory* (to varying degrees not differentiated in the table). Test concerning all young men, generally 19 years of age, administered at the time of military recruitment. Leaving the severely disabled and absentees aside, the entire generation was covered, including young men later to be deemed unfit for military service.

2. Canton in which the total number of young men obtaining the grades of 1 (good) or 2 (acceptable) is proportionally the highest in the subject and year studied. Not necessarily the same canton, depending on the subject and the period (1879 and 1913).

3. The opposite: the lowest total percentage of grades 1 and 2.

Switzerland on the threshold of life had a generally very acceptable real level of education, as Table 1 shows.

In the most advanced cantons, the proportion of satisfactory results approached 100% with regard to reading comprehension, and was around 90% for composition and arithmetic. It was only slightly lower for history, geography and political institutions. The least developed cantons, whose initial level was low, made especially rapid progress during this period, so that in 1913 the results they obtained were far less different from those of the more advanced cantons and from the national average than they were in 1879.

Towards the end of this period, progress continued to be made, but less rapidly than previously, both in the most advanced cantons and nationally. The gap to be bridged at that time must have been particularly difficult. It consisted in allowing young people who were most likely among the most disfavoured to get beyond a certain limit. In the least advanced cantons, the rate of progress remained rapid until the last tests of this kind were administered.

During the same period, the formal level of education of young people had also progressed markedly. In 1887, for example, 17% of recruits had continued their studies beyond the compulsory level. In 1913, that figure had nearly doubled to 32%.

Another phase of progress: the inter-war period in the United States

At the time of the First and Second World Wars, the intellectual level of recruits into the American army was evaluated by means of the Army Alpha Test. The test consisted of several sections: problems in arithmetic, scrambled sentences which had to be put back into the proper order mentally and evaluated as either true or false; series of numbers to be completed after establishing the pattern which determined their order; pairs of words to be classified as synonyms or antonyms; questions requiring common sense. Some questions set in these tests demanded knowledge of physical science, history and geography. Good reading comprehension was required in order to understand some of the more difficult questions (Yoakum & Yerkes, 1920).

This test thus required that the subject make use of his reasoning ability, vocabulary, reading comprehension, knowledge of arithmetic and of facts of various kinds.

Table 2: General education. Arithmetic, basic spelling and grammar, languages. Percentage of twenty-year-old men achieving satisfactory scores according to two surveys: 1975 and 1984, in Switzerland.[1]

	1975	1985
Arithmetic	68.2	45.2
Basic spelling and grammar	77.9	83.1
German (as a second national language. Recruits of French mother-tongue).	24.1	27.0
German (as a second national language. Recruits of Italian mother-tongue).	24.8	33.7
French (as a second national language. Recruits of German mother-tongue).	30.8	31.7
French (as a second national language. Recruits of Italian mother-tongue).	45.1	61.1
Italian (as a second national language. Recruits of German mother-tongue).	5.8	6.0
Italian (as a second national language. Recruits of French mother-tongue).	6.1	10.2
English (recruits of German mother-tongue).	25.6	32.6
English (recruits of French mother-tongue).	18.5	28.7
English (recruits of Italian mother-tongue).	6.6	18.3

1. Girod et al. (1987). Survey concerning recruits. Same items in 1975 and 1984. *Arithmetic*: satisfactory; in a problem involving percentages, made the initial addition and found the correct answer. *Basic spelling and grammar*: agreement of verbs (satisfactory, two-thirds of the items correctly answered). *Languages*: satisfactory; stated that he was able to read the given language (not his mother tongue) fluently, well, or fairly well. Those responding that they were able to read a little or very little are not included. On this point, see note 7 at the end of the chapter. In 1984, the survey also included reading exercises in the second and third national language and in English. The scores obtained with regard to these exercises result in distributions which correspond to those based on stated abilities.

The 1917-18 recruits who did very well on this test were relatively few (4 to 5%). The spread of scores for the others went from this high level of achievement down to the poorest levels.

Between the First and the Second World Wars, the average score of young soldiers went from 69 to 101 points. According to these results, the inter-war period appears to have been an effective period of progress in general education in the United States (Jencks et al, 1972; Stedman & Kaestle, 1986).

This progress coincided with the very marked increase in the level of formal education of young people in the same period: high-school graduates represented only 11.75% of all 17-year-old boys and girls in 1914, but in 1940 that figure had reached 49.0%.

Recent progress in specific subjects

The spread of knowledge is obviously facilitated by the evolution of everyday life. In a contemporary context, such is the case in the use of English outside English-speaking countries.

Table 2 illustrates this trend based on two surveys involving young Swiss adults (20-21 years old for the most part) performing their first period of military service (basic training). These surveys were carried out in 1975 and 1984 respectively.

The progress of computer science is also not surprising. This phenomenon must certainly be occurring in a large number of countries. The bottom line of Table 3 shows just how rapid this evolution has been in the United States among 17-year-olds, within only five years (1978-82).

According to Table 2, knowledge of a second or third national language (German, French, Italian) in Switzerland had also progressed. It is indicative of the interdependence in the evolution of needs and knowledge that such progress was particularly strong among male adolescents in the small Italian-speaking minority. The ability to communicate with customers, suppliers and tourists from other parts of Switzerland, and to handle documents in the language of these regions, is even more valuable to members of this minority than to their compatriots whose mother tongue is one of the country's two dominant languages. It is well known that the proportion of persons who learn a second language tends, for these reasons, to be stronger among members of a linguistic group who are not in a position of dominance than among their compatriots whose language is predominant (Siguan & Mackey, 1986).

Progress can also be observed in subjects which are not related to economic necessity as closely as those just mentioned. An exception of this kind can be seen in Table 2. It shows a slight drop from 1975 to 1984 in Switzerland in the percentage of young men who did not perform satisfactorily in extremely elementary spelling exercises and grammar.

Plateaux

There are some periods of *status quo* and, if observations are repeated at short intervals, it will be seen that they are accompanied by minor oscillations.

In the United States, many highschool graduates, towards the age of 18 in general, take entrance tests in order to enrol in a higher education institution (college). The most common of these tests - in 1970, 1.6 million applicants took it - is the SAT (Scholastic Aptitude Test). It is a direct descendent of the Army Alpha Test (Buros, 1972). The SAT contains two parts: 'mathematics' (the exercises do not exceed the 14-15 year-old level) and 'verbal' (reading comprehension, sentence completion, antonyms, analogies). See Gruber & Bramson (1983) and College Board (1986).

The series of average scores obtained at the national level from 1952 are presented in various publications. These data are well known. Figure 1 (average scores on each part of the test) gives the curve for the years 1952-86. The level remained more or less stable for around a decade (1952-63). This was already inconsistent with the on-going trend towards higher levels of formal education.

Other data from the United States (Table 3) show that from 1971 to 1984 the level of all 17-year-old students remained practically unchanged with regard to reading comprehension. The composition level for students of the

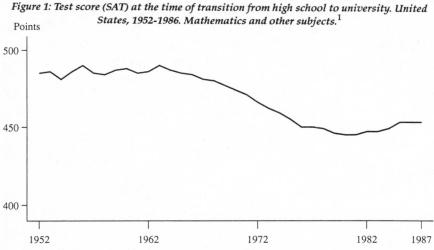

Figure 1: Test score (SAT) at the time of transition from high school to university. United States, 1952-1986. Mathematics and other subjects.[1]

1. Average SAT score (Scholastic Aptitude Test). Highschool graduates wishing to enrol at university (college). Results according to the mathematical and 'verbal' (essentially reading comprehension) forms of the test. Both sexes. According to Austin and Garber (1982); *Statistical abstract of the United States* and 'Facts on file' information bulletins from 1985-1988. The test is optional. Not all university applicants take it. In 1952, the test was taken by 81,200 candidates; in 1962, by 802,500; in 1972, by 1,495,900; in 1977, by 1,401,900.

Table 3. General education. 17-year-old students. United States, 1969-1984[1]

	A. At the beginning of the time-span	B. Intermediate phase	C. At the end of the time-span	Difference A-C
Reading comprehension	68.9 (1971)	69.0 (1975) 68.2 (1980)	69.0 (1984)*	+0.1
Mathematics	55.0 (1973)	52.1 (1978)	51.8 (1982)	-3.2
Science	44.6 (1969)	42.3 (1973) 39.9 (1977)	37.9 (1982)*	-6.7
Composition	A reduction difficult to quantify in the intermediate phase, followed by a return to the same level as the outset. According to 1969, 1974, 1979 and 1984 surveys.			0
Computer science[2]		27.8 (1978)	40.6 (1982)	+12.8

*Estimate

1. Mean percentage of correct responses. Nationwide polls. Same exercises at different dates. National Assessment of Educational Progress: Reports 11-R-01 (1981), 15-R-01 (1985), 13-MA-1 (1983), 08-S-00 (1978), 15-W-01 (1985); Hueftle, Rakow, Welch (1983); Mullis, Oldefendt, Philips (1977); *Social indicators* (USA), 1976.
2. Mean percentage of affirmative answers to five questions: 1. Do you know how to program? 2. Have you ever used a computer to solve a mathematical problem? 3. Have you ever written a program to solve a mathematical problem? 4. Have you ever used a computer to play games? 5. Have you ever written a program for a computer game? NAEP, report 13-MA-01.

same age was more or less the same in 1982 as that of 1969. During the interval it had dropped.

The figures contained in Table 3 come from surveys of the NAEP (National Assessment of Educational Progress), a body which was specially created to prepare statistical indicators on real levels of education. Its observations began in 1969. They mostly concern 9-, 13- and 17-year-old pupils. Sometimes, however, they also include young adults.

According to these figures, it seems that the educational level of young adults (between 26 and 35 years old) in reading comprehension also remained relatively stable between 1971 and 1977 (Brown & Bowditch, 1979).

Declines

According to the SAT, the *status quo* period in the United States mentioned above was followed by a period of steady decline from 1964 to 1980. In 1980, the average score for both parts of the test was 445 points. Twice during the period 1952-65 it recorded 490 points (1956 and 1963). The graph peaks at these points. In comparison, the 45 point drop in 1980 is therefore significant.

This uninterrupted 14-year decline sparked intense debate and gave rise to many analyses. These analyses indicate that the large increase in the proportion of graduates - and, consequently, in test-takers - partially explains the first phase of the decline in the early 1970s: among the applicants there were, no doubt, greater numbers of mediocre students than previously. But afterwards this factor played a minor role.

Moreover, even the absolute number of applicants obtaining a high score (600 points or more) dropped during this period. Other tests, used intensively at the time of transition from secondary school to university, confirm the overall decline in level revealed by the SAT (Austin & Gardner, 1982).

The 1981 mean SAT score was equal to that of the previous year; for the first time since 1966, there had not been a drop from one year to the next. In 1987, however, the SAT score was still very low compared with what it been twenty or thirty years earlier. It is on the basis of such information that it has been said that the United States, rather than elevating an entire generation to a degree of education and skill surpassing that of their parents, was, for the first time in its history, experiencing the opposite phenomenon (Gardner, 1983).

According to Table 3, the level in mathematics and science of 17-year-old students as a group dropped between 1970 and 1982. The NAEP surveys show, moreover, that the level of elementary scientific knowledge of young adults (26 to 35 years old) had also declined between 1973 and 1977 (NAEP, report 08-5-21, 1979).

In Switzerland, as we mentioned earlier in connection with the objectives of primary education, the attainment of at least an acceptable level by nearly all youngsters (male) was once within reach. If the upward trend of the time had been sustained, even at a somewhat slower pace - the final phases always being the most difficult - this goal would have been reached by now.

But the process began to weaken. The 1984 survey mentioned above included a certain number of exercises copied from the 1879-1913 tests. These exercises make it possible to make worthwhile comparisons in the case of arithmetic and reading comprehension. They provide less definite points of reference with respect to history, geography and knowledge of political institutions.

In the case of arithmetic, the percentage of recruits whose level was satisfactory in 1984 varies from 45.2% (grading according to criteria commonly applied by schools),[2] to 70.5% (lenient grading system).[3] On average, the proportion of 1984 recruits who were able to solve the various problems was 48.7%. These three estimates, even the most lenient, fall below the proportion of recruits whose scores were considered satisfactory in 1913. Two of them are even lower than the number of recruits judged to have a satisfactory level in 1879.

In reading comprehension, in 1984, the proportion of recruits of satisfactory level was as follows: 59.1%, according to commonly used criteria; 81.2 % according to lenient criteria; 65.1%, where the average number of correct responses per question is concerned. Here again, the three grading methods resulted in percentages below the 1913 scores, and two of them, below those of 1879.

The exercises were similar, but the means of recording the responses differed (formerly, individual oral examination on the basis of which a grade was assigned; in 1984, completion of a common questionnaire, after which the number of correct answers was counted).

Table 4: Percentage of twenty-year-old men achieving satisfactory scores in elementary arithmetic and reading comprehension (elementary). Switzerland. Long-term trend[1]

	1879	1913	1984
Arithmetic	55	78	55 (45-71)
Reading comprehension	67	91	69 (59-81)

1. 1879 and 1913, Table 1. 1984, average of three grading systems mentioned above, with, in parentheses, that which yields the lowest percentage of those tested achieving a satisfactory score and that which gives the highest.

The comparisons between 1879 and 1984, therefore, are approximate. But in any case, the level of the exercises was modest and, the formal degree of education of the 1984 recruits being quite high, nearly all of these young men should have performed well, no matter what technique was used in the survey.

Such was not the case. Table 4 sums up the results obtained, in rounded figures, when the 1984 results are compared with those from the past.

It appears that there has been more or less a return to the point of departure. In other words, the twentieth century seems ultimately to have undone, rather than to have carried on, all the progress made in the late nineteenth and early twentieth centuries.

In the case of reading comprehension, there is no intermediate reference point making it possible to pinpoint the exact moment at which the trend was reversed. In the case of arithmetic, partial data from the 1975 survey suggest that the point of balance could have been recent (see Table 2).

With regard to geography and history, there has no doubt been a decline compared to 1913, according to the data we possess. Knowledge of political institutions - barely touched upon in 1984 - seems to be situated at about the same level as in 1913. For these three subjects taken as a block, the 1984 level seems to fall between that of 1879 and 1913.

Assessing the current situation

With regard to the subjects contained in all compulsory school curricula, from the primary level upwards, it is possible to adopt relatively precise criteria for evaluating the current situation as the culmination of the trends we have just been describing. Specifically, this involves reading comprehension, elementary mathematics, composition, basic geography, history and science.

For subjects such as computer science and languages, taught in only a fraction of schools at the compulsory level or, in some cases (English in Switzerland, for example), only in specific schools at the post-compulsory level, making an assessment is more difficult.

Normally, with regard to the first group of subjects in countries in which the vast majority of today's youngsters continue their studies several years beyond the compulsory stage (including apprenticeships combining general courses with practical experience), most adults of around 20 years of age or a little older should possess levels which could be qualified as 'good', or at least - let us not be overly optimistic - quite 'acceptable'. Some of the foregoing indications, those which cannot be reduced to a score, but which - as is the case with the Swiss data - derive from an estimate of the percentage of individuals whose level is deemed to be satisfactory, clearly show that such is not the case.

We will now examine this point in greater depth, beginning with the United States. The indications which follow are drawn from a nationwide survey conducted in 1985 concerning the so-called 'literacy' rate of young men and women aged 21 to 25. Since previous studies on a similar subject do not exist, we were not able to refer to this survey in the foregoing discussion. It is nonetheless particularly suitable as an indication of the current situation in a major, developed country on the threshold of the twenty-first century.

Here we will define the literacy rate (or the level of general education) as the 'ability to make use of printed and written information to function in

Examples illustrating the real educational level of young adults (United States, 1985)

I. Knowing how to calculate the total monthly interest and total cumulative interest
on a credit purchase: 9%

II. Understanding, for example, a newspaper article on genetic manipulations or on
the subtler details about an incident which occurred in Asia and is causing international tensions upon which the entire world is commenting: 9%

III. Understanding a document on systems of remuneration and explaining what differentiates two of them: 9%

IV. Ability to read a timetable to determine the departure time of a bus going from
one place to another, in the middle of a Saturday afternoon, on a line which does
not run at the same intervals on weekends as during the week: 20%

V. Calculating how much change they receive if they give three dollars at a cafeteria
to pay for a bowl of soup ($0.60, according to the menu) and a sandwich ($1.95),
and how much they should leave as a tip, if the tip is 10%: 23%

VI. Using a city map to find the way from one location to another: 57%

VII. Knowing how to write a letter to point out an error in a bill: 72%

VIII. Interpreting a pay slip: 73%

IX. Knowing how to write a check to pay the amount indicated on a bill: 83%

X. Finding the sum of two deposits figuring on a bank statement: 92%

XI. Filling out a job application: 96%

XII. Ability to find the time of a television programme in a newspaper: 96%

XIII. Knowing how to enter a telephone number on an index card: 98%

XIV. Identifying the expiry date on a driver's license and knowing what it means: 98%

XV. Ability to sign their name in the proper place on an identity card: 99.7%

---

society and achieve one's goals, and to develop one's knowledge and
potential' (NAEP, reports 16-PL-01 and 16-PL-02). This definition has the
usual (and perhaps incurable) vagueness of all attempts at defining 'functional literacy'.

Examination of the contents of the questionnaire will make its goals
clearer, however. It concentrated mainly on elements of general education,
which it evaluated by means of exercises based on everyday situations
which adults must regularly confront: understanding newspaper and ma-
gazine articles; commenting on them; using documents containing practical
information (schedules, bank statements, pay slips, etc.); writing letters;
filling out administrative forms or cards to pass on information in a work-

related situation; performing very simple calculations, such as when paying bills.

The above box gives a few examples of the exercises used, together with the approximate percentages of those who answered correctly. Those at the top of the list are among the 'most difficult' of the survey. Those which follow descend in order of difficulty to the most elementary.

On the basis of just over 100 varied exercises of this kind, the persons questioned were classified according to a scale ranging from 0 to 500 points. Classification was made according to three kinds of exercise: (a) comprehension, explanation and drafting of routine texts (reading an article, writing a letter, etc.); (b) use of documents containing practical information (schedules, city maps, catalogues, filling out a card, etc.); (c) common calculations (involving a bank statement, etc.).

The overall distribution of those surveyed is very similar from these points of view, although at the individual level, the correlation between the three kinds of skills is only moderate. We calculated the average of the three categories. The figure is given in Table 5. Here, young American adults are

Table 5. General education (literacy). Young adults, 21-25 years old (both sexes). United States, 1985[1]

Level[2]	Distribution	Cumulative percentage
A. Acceptable (or higher)	9.0	9.0
B. Fair	47.5	56.5
C. Mediocre	39.5	96.0
D. Poor	3.7	99.7
E. Very poor	0.3	100
Total%	100	

1. National Assessment of Educational Progress. I S Kirsch et al. *Literacy: profiles of America's young adults: final report.* Approximaterly 250 p. plus annexes. Sept. 1986. Report 16-PL-01. Princeton. *Literacy: profiles of America's young adults,* summary. Same authors, NAEP, Report 16-PL-02, 68 pages, 1986.
2. *Level A*: Acceptable level of general education, probably corresponding to the principle objectives of compulsory school curricula. Knowledge of the level of examples 1-3 in the text; *Level B*: Knowledge of the level of examples 4-6; *Level C*: Knowledge of the level of examples 7-10; *Level D*: Knowledge of the level of examples 11-14; *Level E*: Knowledge of the level of example 15.

assigned to five levels which we have defined and labelled. The notes below the table indicate the type of skill corresponding to each of these levels.

Those at Level A displayed a degree of general education which can be qualified as at least acceptable. But, let us emphasize that those surveyed and who rank at this level only represent those who were able to perform the highest level exercises easily in a survey which, all things considered, had nothing to do with education in the humanistic sense of the word. To be ranked at level A, it was sufficient to comprehend articles and other very ordinary messages, to perform very common practical calculations correctly, etc. In short, these individuals represent those who, among those tested, find themselves at the supposed level of the general public, of the majority of workers, of ordinary customers, and the majority of the intensive users of social services.

It is at this level that most young adults raised in a highly advanced society and, thus the product of a highly developed education system, should find themselves. Many young adults should score well above this modest threshold. Yet, in the United States, it is not the majority of young adults who rank at level A, but a small minority of them: less than one-tenth.

Others more or less approach this level. They represent (level B) slightly less than half the total. The remainder of the generation are situated at levels which are unquestionably unsatisfactory (levels C-E). But, nonetheless, very few of them are totally illiterate.

Other observations made in the United States corroborate what has just been said.[5] With regard to reading comprehension, precise comparisons show that the young adults of the 1985 survey score somewhat higher than students aged 17 (Kirsch & Jugeblut, 1986). What we have just pointed out, therefore, may be considered to be a faithful reflection of reality and not a distortion of it.

In Switzerland, the situation is probably not much different, at least if the results of the exercise related to reading comprehension, arithmetic, elementary mathematics, history, geography, etc. are an indication. Inclusion of another category of knowledge - languages - however, brings out aspects of the real level of education of young adults which are much less disappointing. A series of examples illustrating this are given in Table 6.

According to the ten examples given in the table, only four out of ten Swiss young adults attain or surpass the 'fair' level, deemed here to be satisfactory. The survey comprised still other exercises pertaining to the same fields or fields similar to those used in these examples. All exercises combined, the proportion of those tested achieving a score deemed satisfac-

Table 6. Examples illustrating the real level of young adults (Switzerland, 1984). Reading comprehension, basic spelling and grammar, art and literature, practical information.

Level	Unsatisfactory	Satisfactory Appr. 2/3 or more of the exercises correct	Total (%)
Reading comprehension			
– Short texts of primary school level.	40	60	100
– Excerpts of an article from a travel magazine and of information sent by the government to all voters.	63	37	100
– A short text of primary school level, followed by more difficult readings, but taken from publications destined for the general public.	72	28	100
Basic spelling and grammar	19	81	100
Mathematics			
– Arithmetic (problems of primary school level).	55	45	100
– Equations, angles, sets in particular (13-year-old pupils).	68	32	100
History and geography			
– Geography (Swiss mountain chains, the cantons linked by the Gothard).	67	33	100
– History (great turning points in Swiss history; give the date, within ten years, of the Wall Street stock market crash, of Hitler's accession to power and other importantevents in the twentieth century).	82	18	100
Art and literature			
– Michelangelo, Mozart, Botticelli, Picasso, etc. (were they painters or composers? Their period, within two centuries). Dante, Tolstoy, Hemingway, Chaplin etc. (identify one of their works from a list of titles). Thirty-threequestions.	91	9	100
Practical information			
– On the basis of a leaflet issued to rail travellers, take note of the reduced rates available for certain types of journeys and calculate their respective prices.	65	35	100
Average based on these examples.	62	38	100

tory is slightly higher than when the ten examples presented above are considered by themselves. The proportion is 45%. Also, if the average is calculated for all exercises combined with the exception of the questions related to art and literature - which proved to be catastrophic - the proportion rises to 52%.

In any case, this is far below a result attesting to a level of education which would be expected of Switzerland in view of its very high national income and other indicators of the country's modern character, not the least of which is the size of its education system and the means it has at its disposal.

The majority of those tested did not limit their studies to compulsory education. Nearly all of them went on either to apprenticeships which included class attendance or to more advanced secondary education.[6]

Let us take a look at language studies. Switzerland is a plurilingual country. But very few inhabitants are bilingual, or even able to take part in a business discussion or a political debate, etc., in a national language other than their own without difficulty. Yet, many can more or less cope in a second language.[7] This situation, though not ideal, appears nonetheless to be quite satisfactory when viewed realistically, unlike the situation reflected by the level observed with regard to other subjects covered by the 1984 survey.

Remarks

Many diverse present trends tending towards many different levels would no doubt become discernible, on the basis of - let us reiterate - sufficiently numerous observations.[8]

In particular, it would be important to see whether developing countries are currently in the process of improving the real level of knowledge in the areas which make up the foundation of general education or whether in these countries, as in the two countries discussed in this chapter, there is stagnation or even regression in this regard. Unfortunately, we cannot answer this and a great many other questions, for lack of data.

The real level of knowledge - or the true state of the 'human capital' everywhere proclaimed as the most precious resource of nations - remains for the most part undetermined.

If we take the risk of combining the American and Swiss data related to the long-term evolution, an approach which is certainly open to criticism, it appears possible to acknowledge that distinct progress was made with regard to the dissemination of general education until about the mid-twentieth century.

This progress seems to have given way to stagnation with regard to verbal skills (reading and composition), and to a decline with regard to mathematics and science, geography, history. In contrast, progress is to be noted in other fields. From the data upon which our remarks are based, only computer science (the United States) and languages (Switzerland) show evidence of such progress.

At present, in the subjects which are currently stagnating or declining, the level of a large percentage of young adults (or 'pre-adults') is low or mediocre. It is just barely acceptable in a more-or-less equivalent number of cases. Only a fraction are situated at a level genuinely compatible with the goals of compulsory education. Only a small number of these surpass this level, a rather modest result, all things considered.

A generation's *formal* level of general education is not, as we have seen, of much value in representing the *real* level of knowledge of the members of that generation. In the case of countries in which an evolution of the latter is perceptible, it seems only to have kept pace with the formal level of days gone by.

In discussions concerning the evolution of the real level of education, the changes most often mentioned are declines. In the United States, in particular, the declines are reflected in SAT and other similar test scores into 1980, in addition to declines with regard to certain subjects (including stagnation at a very low level in others) as revealed by the NAEP. The recent modest improvement of SAT scores and kindred tests has introduced a new element into the debate.

Elsewhere, data are generally totally non-existent or come in the form of fragmentary indications, so that opinions collide in the greatest confusion.

Table 7 makes possible certain observations regarding the context in which the trends noted in this chapter are taking place. Concerning the United States, the points of reference it provides are derived from indications made available by global tests (Army Alpha Test, SAT) and from the results of the NAEP survey concerning two basic subjects: reading comprehension and arithmetic (and other branches of mathematics). The Swiss data contained in this table also relate to these two subjects. In addition, the table provides more recent indications pertaining to computer science (United States) and English (Switzerland) For other subjects (composition, geography, history, science), we may refer to the text. Their inclusion in Table 7 would not change what follows.

Eight generations are included in this table. They illustrate particularly significant features in the trends observed. The first two (A and B) belong

Table 7. Overview (1900-1084)

Generation (country)	Birth date	When age 5-15	Evolution					Situation			
			Global scores	Reading	Math	Computer science	English	Reading	Math	Computer science	English
A. Age 20 in 1900 (Switzerland)	1880	1885-95	*	+	+	*	*	G	G	*	*
B. Age 20 in 1943 (United States)	1923	1928-38	+	*	*	*	*	*	*	*	*
C. Age 18 in 1960 (United States)	1942	1947-57	#	*	*	*	*	*	*	*	*
D. Age 18 in 1965 (United States)	1947	1952-62	-	*	*	*	*	*	*	*	*
E. Age 18 in 1980 (United States)	1962	1967-77	-	*	*	*	*	*	*	*	*
F. Age 18 in 1981-85 (United States)	1963-67	1968-82	+	#	-	+	*	M	M	G	*
G. Age 21-25 in 1985 (United States)	1960-64	1965-79	*	*	*	*	*	M	M	*	*
H. Age 20 in 1984 (Switzerland)	1964	1969-79	*	-	-	*	+	M	M	*	G

+ = improvement; G = good; - = decline; M = mediocre, poor; # = no change; * = unknown to the erstwhile phase of progress (Switzerland and the United States). The third (C) is taken from among the plateau generations, whose level is comparatively acceptable, as observed in the United States between 1952 and 1963 on the basis of global tests.

Generation A grew up in the late nineteenth century; a period, to be sure, of sustained economic growth in Switzerland, yet the conditions in which large portions of the population lived were nonetheless difficult.

At the close of the nineteenth century, the real national income in Switzerland was about five times less than it is today. Education was developing. The minority that pursued its studies beyond the compulsory level was growing. But it remained a minority nevertheless. Thus, the generations whose progress is reflected in Table 1 were brought up in a context which is extremely remote from the 'era of prosperity' and the phase of the universalization of post-primary studies in Switzerland.

Generation B is the generation of young American soldiers of the Second World War era. Their score on the Army Alpha Test proved to be higher than that of their 1917-18 predecessors. Yet, generation B, born in 1923, was in the classroom during the Great Depression, and lived through the tensions and hardships of the 1930s.

This generation was not, therefore, born to easy times. Quite the contrary.

Paradoxically, with the relief and prosperity of the post-war years, the pace at which the real level of education rose was not stepped up, if SAT scores are an indication. The new climate - in which Generation C grew up - seems on the contrary to have brought the upward trend to a halt. In the United States, the generations schooled at the time of the economic boom of 1950s and 1960s, which was also a period of considerable development for education, are already among those who belong to the phase of falling SAT scores (example: Generation D).

This decline continued into the post-campus revolt generations of the mid-1970s. This is also the era of the Vietnam War and of the 1974-75 economic recession. Feeble signs of improvement of SAT scores nonetheless became visible with generations having lived in a somewhat similar context (Generation F). For these generations, NAEP surveys also indicated stagnations (reading comprehension, in particular), declines (mathematics, especially), but also an improvement (computer science). The individuals under Generation G are from the 1985 American survey concerning the general level of education of young adults. They make up generations E and F.

The Switzerland of the past few decades - prosperous, at peace, untroubled by unemployment, endowed with a dense network of well-equipped schools - is currently producing generations of young adults (case H) whose real level of education appears to be lower than that of their great-grandparents in areas such as reading comprehension, arithmetic, history and geography. For these subjects, the situation, which was good or fair at the beginning of this century, has now become mediocre or poor. But, in the case of languages, these same generations are ahead of the young adults of 1975.

Thus, the advent of the consumer society and the democratization of education have indeed engendered unexpected stagnations and declines, but at the same time improvements. It is extremely likely that progress would be noted elsewhere if studies were extended to typical modern forms of knowledge: all areas which relate to entertainment and other new forms of leisure activities, for example, tourism.

All in all, there has been neither only regression nor only progress on all fronts, but rather, movement in different directions. This is certainly true for all periods, though things no doubt evolve with breathtaking speed in this age of accelerated change in technology, social structures, ways of living and of thinking.

With regard to the progress made by computer science and English, the likely explanation is obvious. We are dealing here with skills which in our modern civilization are deemed more useful and the number of opportunities to make use of them is greater. More and more individuals take an interest in these subjects (reinforcement of motivation) as soon as they reach school age. Later on, many feel the need for refresher training. The retention and extension of acquired knowledge are fostered by how frequently this knowledge is made use of (repetition, exercise).

To satisfy this growing demand, more ad hoc forms of education, both public and private, are offered. More and more people enrol in such courses, generally to good advantage. What we have seen with regard to the especially distinct progress in the knowledge of national languages in the - minority - Italian part of Switzerland is another example of the influence of needs.

To appreciate these stagnations and declines fully, it is no doubt necessary to look for similar causes. Indeed, these trends are most likely the result of the amount of interest a society in flux attaches to given forms of knowledge. To the minds of many students, interest in these fields is no longer a foregone conclusion. Outside school and downstream from it, at least for a large number of individuals, there tend to be fewer opportunities to make use of the knowledge acquired, so that the benefits derived from education fail to fructify or are slowly eroded away.

The example of the drop of the level in arithmetic in this regard is poignant. Progress in electronics, which is at the origin of the more wide-spread mastery of computer skills, also renders (thanks to pocket calcula-tors, keyboards in offices, shops, banks, etc.) the need to rely on 'manual' calculation less important. The degree of usefulness - or intrinsic intellectual interest - of knowledge about history, geography, science, algebra, geometry, etc., is probably on the decline. It is not entirely impossible - although this is more surprising - that the same applies to reading in general, as well as to the understanding of printed sources of practical information. This is one of the numerous points which remain to be elucidated.

Whereas the evolution of the population's level in various branches of knowledge, and hence, the level at any given time, is certainly a function of the evolution of the effective degree of interest they generate, other factors are involved. Those most frequently invoked relate to the declines, whether real or presumed (particularly that of SAT scores through 1980 in the United States).

As far as schools are concerned, specific mention is made of: the relaxing of screening criteria and of discipline; the arrival in secondary level classes of students whose degree of motivation and preparation varies; the medio-crity of certain textbooks; the decreasing prestige and authority of teaching staff or the inadequate training of teachers; improvised reforms and experi-ments.

With regard to society's responsibilities, the following culprits are sin-gled out: the higher divorce rate; the arrival of waves of underprivileged immigrant workers whose children frequently have difficulty keeping up in school, for both linguistic and other reasons; changes in the scale of values; decline in morals; unemployment; poverty, both old and new; and also the overabundance of goods, of gadgets, of forms of entertainment in many households; the excessively facile mode of existence they enjoy and the laziness this encourages; television (it has been calculated that in the United States, by the time they are 16, the majority of adolescents will have spent between 10,000 and 15,000 hours in front of the television, that is, more than in school); drugs, delinquency, the 'baby boom' (large families being sus-pected by a certain ideological movement of being poorer educators than small ones), etc.

It is reasonable to assume that some of these factors do play a role. The incidence of some of them on the inequality of student achievements has been confirmed. However, the cause-effect relationship which might exist between such factors and the trends we have seen or the present level of entire generations of young adults is still unresolved (Austin & Garber, 1982).

To go beyond these suppositions, we must precisely determine - and produce convincing evidence of - both the role of the factors which are among the causes of the low level reached in this century in certain subjects and the incidence which other factors, or the same factors in different circumstances, have had on current progress, or yet again, that which they had on progress of the past.

Notes

1. Percentage of highschool graduates among 18 year olds (of both sexes): 1950: 56.0; 1960 72.4; 1970: 77.1 (record); 1980: 71.4: 1983: 71.8.

2. Satisfactory result = around two-thirds of the items or more of an exercise completed correctly. Thus, in scholastic terms, a grade between 4 and 6 in Switzerland, or 13 and 20, etc.

3. Satisfactory result = around half of the items or more in the exercise performed correctly.

4. As mentioned below: more than nine-tenths of those tested in 1984 had attended school beyond the compulsory level.

5. Concerns all adults and not only young adults In particular, the well-known estimates of the Adult Performance Level Project, according to which around 20% of adults are functional illiterates, that is, extremely under-educated in comparison to demands of private and professional life in an advanced society. Since these demands are defined in various ways, this proportion varies depending on the survey. Many concrete indications exist concerning aspects of the real level of the knowledge of adults quoted by Stedman & Kaestle (1986, p.99 et seq.).

6. Compulsory education only or incomplete post compulsory education, 8%; post-compulsory schooling sanctioned by a diploma or an anticipated diploma, 92%.

7. Recruits of German mother tongue (1984) stating that they were able to read French (percentages): 'very well': 2.3; 'well', 12.3; 'quite well', 17.0; 'a little', 20.3; 'very little', 21.0; 'not at all', 22.3%; missing responses (which, allowing for exceptions, actually also signifies 'not at all'), 4.8. The break-down of all recruits with regard to English is about the same. It is roughly similar for German (where recruits of French or Italian mother tongue are concerned). However, it differs appreciably with regard to knowledge of French on the part of Italian-speaking recruits ('very well', 7.1; 'well', 26.7; 'quite well', 27.3; 'a little', 20.7; 'very little', 10.1; 'not at all', 2.4; missing responses, 5.9).

8. For example, the improvement in military recruitment tests in France accomplished over approximately the past thirty years (Baudelot & Establet, 1988).

CHAPTER TWO

Social background, schooling and real level of general education

The motivations, means and opportunities to learn are not equally distributed among all social classes. The same is true of factors which affect knowledge negatively, which stifle the desire to learn, hinder its realization or favour the forgetting of what has been learned.

What is more, at compulsory grade levels, students are already often separated into advanced and less advanced classes, into sections, not to mention the inequality which can exist between rural and urban schools, between schools in upper-class neighbourhoods and in poorer neighbourhoods. Post-compulsory training is provided via different channels. Such training ranges from very short to extremely thorough apprenticeship programmes, from the least selective high school classes to the most selective, from the least ambitious university programmes to those with the most elevated goals; not forgetting those individuals who get jobs immediately after compulsory schooling and those who drop out of post-compulsory programmes before obtaining a diploma. All of these differences will invariably affect the level of both specialized (professional qualifications, in particular) and general knowledge.

As in the preceding chapter, we will concern ourselves here with knowledge as it applies to general education.

If reality were as simple as many would have it be, the situation about to be discussed would look very much like Figure 2.

'Social class', defined according to the economic status of the parents (C), would determine almost entirely the type of schooling (S), which in turn would completely define the nature and level of knowledge, in particular,

Figure 2: Relationship between social origin, type of studies and level of general education: inaccurate model

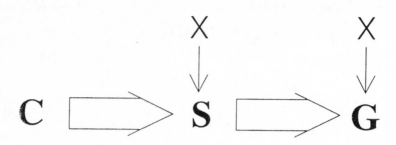

of general culture (G). Other factors (X) would nonetheless be responsible for a certain proportion of exceptions, consisting in particular of a small percentage of very bright students of working-class origin, who escape the common fate of youngsters of their social background.

In fact, reality is different from this scheme of things. Very different.

The factors determining an individual's level of knowledge are numerous. One factor is the influence exerted by the nature and duration of schooling. Yet this factor is far from being determinant. The influence of differences in standards of living and life styles which the division of the population into social classes or more or less analogous categories attempts to reflect is even less determinant.

The diagram which better illustrates the real relationship between social background, schooling and real degree of general education, rather than the one given above, would be Figure 3.

Social class (C) does not determine schooling (S). It only exerts a certain influence on it (a) of which it only very partially explains the course. Because of this or because of the educative influence (b) it exerts independently of the school, social class again only very partially explains the general level of education (G). For its part, formal schooling (S), meanwhile, only partly conditions (c) the general level of education. Although far more limited than is commonly held, the influence of this component is nonetheless markedly greater than that of social background. Both schooling and the level of

Figure 3. Relationship between social origin, type of studies and real level of general education.

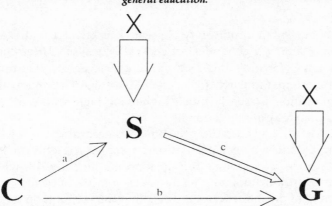

general education depend massively on other factors (X). This is the actual picture.

*   *   *

It was twenty years ago that some excellent work put educational sociology on a new course by resolutely insisting that reality corresponds to the second of the above scenarios, the first being purely utopian.

One of these works was the Coleman Report in the United States (Coleman, 1966) and the first comparative study conducted under the auspices of the International Association for the Evaluation of Educational Achievement (IEA). It focused on mathematics (children 13 years of age and students in the senior year of secondary school) and involved twelve countries (Husén et al., 1967).[1]

A short time later, an important work authored by Christopher Jencks and other authors (Jencks et al., 1972), as well as other studies of the IEA - twenty-two countries, students from 10 to 14 years of age and students in the last year of secondary school, six subjects (Passow et al., 1976; Peaker, 1975; Purves & Levine, ed. 1975; Walker, 1976) - contributed significantly to our understanding of the problem.

The studies of the IEA just mentioned are especially valuable from the point of view of the present work, because of the international comparisons they contain. They remain unparalleled. We will refer extensively to it in this chapter, whilst also borrowing data from other, more recent studies, involving young adults. These data also suggest that social background and type of schooling only explain a minor part of the inequality of effective levels of general education.

* * *

Yet, the inequality of opportunity is great. This chapter will examine the chances of attaining a good level of general education. These chances are markedly lower for individuals of working class origin than for those of upper class origin. Similarly, the probability of demonstrating such a real level of education is clearly much higher for high school or university graduates than for other individuals.

At first sight, fact contradicts the analyses according to which the real level of individuals in general education subjects is only marginally a function of social background and the kind of schooling. We will see that this is not a contradiction, but merely different facets of reality.

The extent of the influence of factors other than schools on the real level of general education of individuals obviously provides an incentive for in-depth revision of ideas about the possibility of changing the distribution and general level of this kind of knowledge through educational reform.

* * *

This chapter is a brief, non-technical overview. It reviews the main aspects of the problem of the impact of social background and type of schooling on the real level of general education of individuals. It is followed by three - methodological - chapters which complement it.

Analysing the share of any factor in the explanation of a given form of inequality (here, the influence of social background and type of schooling in explaining the inequalities in certain kinds of knowledge) is quite a complex operation. It plays a significant role in numerous contemporary works, in the field of educational sociology in particular. We therefore thought it would be useful to explain in considerable detail the nature of this type of analysis and the manner of interpreting the results (Chapters III and IV). Annex C examines, on the basis of genuine examples, how one variable can be at the origin of a very great inequality of opportunity in a given area and only play a minor role from an explanatory point of view. The data referred to in Chapters III, IV and V, as well as in some passages of Chapter II, are contained in an annex.

With regard to content, Chapters III-V are also applicable to the study of the inequality of opportunity according to social background in connection with the educational selection process and for the incidence of schooling on social mobility.

Inequalities

Inequality of the real level of knowledge *per se* (classification of members of a population according to levels of knowledge) and the inequality of opportunity with regard to knowledge (comparison of distribution by levels of knowledge of men versus women, of members of different ethnic groups, or 'races', regions, social classes, etc.) are, of course, virtually nil when the evaluation criteria are not sufficiently strict. If the tests employed to measure knowledge in a given subject were so simple that everyone passed, the proportion of individuals placed in the top category would be 100%, irrespective of their rank in terms of social background or any other criterion.

If the standard is raised only just a little, a notable general degree of inequality appears, as well as an equally notable degree of inequality of opportunity.

The higher the standard is raised, the greater these two forms of inequality become.

Let us take a first example, that of the reading level (reading comprehension) of young 20-year-old males in Switzerland, according to the 1984 study referred to in Chapter I. The figures are contained in the Annex to Chapters II to V.

The exercises were very simple. Theoretically, nearly all young adults should be able to do such exercises very satisfactorily in our day and age and in countries such as Switzerland where most people of the same generation have completed several years of study (including vocational training) beyond the compulsory level or even until the age of 20.

The ceiling category (the 'pass' level shown in the tables in the Annex to Chapters II to V) is set at a modest level. To be placed in this category it was sufficient to complete two-thirds of the exercises correctly. Yet, only one-third of these young men scored at this level. The others fall into categories ranging from very poor to mediocre. The proportion of young men demonstrating a satisfactory level is one-half in the case of the sons of white-collar workers, one-fourth in the case of children of working class parents. The latter therefore are half as likely to demonstrate this level of knowledge (Table 17).

The inequality of opportunity reflects the relationship between, on one hand, the rank of individuals according to characteristics for which they are not responsible because they are imposed at birth (sex, 'colour', parents' social class, etc.) and, on the other hand, what life offers them afterwards.

The effect of the formal level of education, that is, the highest level attained in school, is not relevant to the inequality of opportunity. Indeed, the type of schooling received is an acquired trait, not imposed, although in fact, it owes much, like any other acquired characteristic, to the influence of a series of factors which the individual cannot control.

Table 27 shows, again in connection with the young men in the Swiss study, that the percentage of secondary school graduates having the very modest reading level described above is high, which is normal. Among those of the same generation without a diploma, the proportion of these cases is, on the contrary, low. It is six-times lower.

In the United States, among young adults, the chances of ranking at an acceptable level of general education (level A in Table 5) is fourteen times higher for 'whites' than for 'blacks'. The distinction based on 'colour' in fact is due to differences in social condition and standard of living. The probability of attaining the same acceptable level of general education is purely and simply 'nil' in the case of a small fraction of young American adults who did not get beyond elementary school. With regard to those who traditionally abandon their studies, the classic secondary school 'drop-outs', the probability is five times lower than for secondary school graduates and nearly thirty times lower for college graduates (NAEP, Report 16-PL-02, 1986).

As soon as the ceiling category is raised, the gaps according to social background and formal level of education grow even wider than in the examples just cited.

With regard to children and adolescents still in school, the formal level of education does not come into the picture. It only indicates the endpoint attained in school. One must therefore consider the type of school and section attended by these children and these adolescents.

The disparity of real levels in different subjects of general education is great according to such criteria. It is also significant when examined from the point of view of social background (Coleman, 1966; Bloom, 1976; research of the US Assessment of Educational Progress and of the IEA; Parelius, 1978; Robin & Barrier, 1985, etc.).

Here we are very close to the familiar observations commonly made on the basis, not of the direct evaluation of knowledge by means of tests, but on student achievement in terms of grades or the number of years repeated (among the classics on the subject: Warner et al., 1944; Sauvy & Girard, 1965; more recently: Prost, 1986; Halsey et al., 1980. Numerous analogous works, data collections, such as 'Données sociales', six volumes; 'The condition of education', yearbook; 'Digest of education statistics', yearbook, etc.).

Distributions

Despite the significant inequalities of which we have just seen some examples, the relationship between social background and the kind of current schooling or the formal level of education attained, on one hand, and the real level in certain general education subjects on the other, is in no way absolute in a generation. For this reason the share accounted for by social background, type of current schooling or formal level of education in the explanation of inequalities in real levels of general education is small.

The inputs in the calculation of the shares of causality or explanatory impacts consist of very simple two-way classifications. On the one hand, the members of a generation are ranked according either to an aspect of their social background (social class, for example, or level of formal instruction of their parents, etc.), or according to an aspect of the kind of current studies (type of school, section, nature of the programme in which the student is enroled, teaching methods, etc.), or, in the case of adults, according to their formal level of education. On the other hand, the same individuals are ranked according to their knowledge levels in a given area.

These tables are a very direct reflection of reality. If the study is done properly, they give a true indication of how a generation may be allocated both (a) according to a characteristic relating to their social condition or schooling either current or completed, and (b) according to the knowledge demonstrated via responses to questions or the way exercises are dealt with.

These rankings reveal differences of level for a given category in terms of social background and type of schooling. At the same time, they make it possible to observe to what extent these differences vary positively or negatively according to social background and type of schooling.

This is the result produced by all of the influences at work. These influences are of two kinds:

- those which result in differences in levels of knowledge within a given category consisting of individuals grouped according to social background and type of studies (so-called 'within-group' differences)1;
- those which result in distribution differences by knowledge level, depending on the social background or kind of studies ('between-group' differences).

The two way tables reflect within-group and between-group differences combined. The analysis of the explanatory impacts, on the contrary, consists in dissociating them. For the time-being, we will not concern ourselves with this type of analysis. Instead, we will limit ourselves to two-way distributions. The Annex to Chapters II to V gives two real examples (reading levels according to social class and according to formal levels of education), at age 20.

Here is a hypothetical example which illustrates, in an extremely simplified manner, what we have just said.

In this example, individuals are classified according to a given characteristic (an aspect of their social background or of the type of studies, for example) into two categories (A_1 and A_2). They are also classified according to their level of knowledge in a given field: level I or II.

Each of the two categories A_1 and A_2 include members of levels I and II. Hence, the category does not determine the level. We are dealing here with within-group differences.

But it also appears that the distribution by level varies according to the category. Half of the individuals in group A_1 are at level I and, hence, half are also at level II. In contrast, fewer individuals from the A_2 group are at level II than at level I. This difference in distribution by levels according to category (between-group difference) translates into deviations of the mean scores. The level of the A_1 group is 1.50 points and that of the A_2 group is 1.38. The overall mean is 1.42.

The degree of dependence of the level in relation to category, without distinction between within-group and between-group differences, can by expressed using various indices. In the hypothetical example illustrated in Table 8, one of them indicates a correlation of 0.12.

If the category determined the level, the correlation would be 1. All individuals in A_1 and only those in A_1 would be at level II; and the individuals in A_2 and only those in A_2 would be at level I. All differences would be between-group differences. The average score of the A_1's, in fact

---

Table 8. Hypothetical example

A given trait	Level (score in points)		Total
	I (1 point)	II (2 points)	
A_1	2	2	4
A_2	5	3	8
Total	7	5	12

Mean level: A_1 = 1.50; A_2 = 1.38; Total = 1.42. Correlation (eta) .120.

the score of each of them, would be 2 points. That of the A_2's would be 1 point.

Inversely, if the differences between categories has no effect on differences in level, the correlation would be 0. A_1's and A_2's would be distributed in equal proportions between level I and level II. All differences in level would be within-group differences. The mean score of the A_1's and A_2's would be identical. Possibly, there would be no difference: everyone would be at the same level, either I or II.

The correlation of the hypothetical example given in Table 8 is far closer to what would result from the absence of effect of differences of category on the distribution between levels than the other extreme, that of the absolute dependence of level on category. If the degree of dependence of level in relation to the category were no more than average, the correlation would be of the magnitude of 0.5. That of our hypothetical example is not even quite half of this. It is to this kind of conclusion that real observations ordinarily lead.

The results of such observations vary depending on the country, age and characteristics selected in defining the social background or kind of schooling, the subjects being considered, the nature of tests, the subtlety of the classifications.

The correlations observed are, in general, quite small, sometimes average. Only exceptionally are they greater.

In Switzerland (young men 20 years of age), the correlation social category/level of knowledge is, on the average, based on observations involving eight subjects, 0.148, when those questioned are broken down into three main social classes (working class, middle and upper classes). The average correlation then becomes 0.264, which is still small, when twenty-two types of social background categories are differentiated (Table 30, see page 108). Using this very detailed classification, the correlation by field ranges from 0.2 to 0.24 where the subjects concerned are part of the nucleus of general education (reading comprehension, mathematics, in particular). The highest coefficient concerns English (0.38). But even this peak value is considerably below 0.5, that is, a correlation of average magnitude.

In the case of these young men, the correlation formal level of education/level of knowledge for all eight subjects averages out to 0.359 when those tested are grouped according to only three types of educational background: those not in possession of a diploma; vocational school graduates; secondary school graduates. This average correlation goes to 0.437 when forty-one levels of formal education are differentiated. On the basis

Table 9. *Social background, kind of schooling and real level of knowledge. Correlations. Examples of differences reported according to country, subject, age (13-14 = students 13-14 years old; final = in final year of secondary school)*[1]

	England & Wales		Australia		Japan		Netherlands		United States		India		Average[4]	
	13-14	final	13-14	final	13-14	final	13-14	final	13-14	final	13-14	final	13-14	final
Mathematics[2]														
Social background														
Socio-professional category of the father	0.38	0.08	0.22	0.05	0.25	0.08	0.33	-0.04	0.28	0.24	*	*	0.24	0.08
Formal level of education of the mother	0.24	0.12	0.04	0.03	0.32	0.13	0.27	0	0.29	0.25	*	*	0.18	0.09
Place of residence (rural area, small town etc.)	0.07	0.07	0.05	0	0.2	0.01	0.03	0.2	0.18	0.39	*	*	0.03	0.08
Type of schooling														
Section	0.27	0.19	0.46	0.5	*	*	0.74	*	0.31	0.16	*	*	0.37	0.32
Hours of class per week	0.03	-0.08	-0.01	0.11	0.04	0.15	0.19	-0.01	-0.04	-0.16	*	*	-0.0	0
Educational background of teachers (length of their post-secondary training)	0.32	0.01	0.1	0.1	0.03	0.17	-0.1	0.08	0.08	0.14	*	*	0.08	0.05
Science[2]														
Social background														
Socio-professional category of the father	0.34	0.06	0.24	0.06	0.24	*	0.25	0.09	0.31	0.21	0.13	0.09	0.23	0.09

Formal level of education of the mother	0.20	-0.04	0.19	0.09	0.21	*	0.12	0.02	0.25	0.22	0.04	0.05	0.15	0.08
Family library (number of books)	0.34	-0.01	0.24	0.08	0.32	*	0.12	0.06	0.25	0.16	0.1	0.18	0.21	0.09
Type of schooling														
School (urban, rural, private, public, primary, technical, commercial, classical, etc. high school, various criteria according to the country.	0.51	0.12	0.17	0.04	0.12	*	0.45	0.4	0.12	0.04	0.12	0.03	0.23	0.08

* no data available

1. 1964 survey (Husén, 1967). Thirteen-year-old students and students in the final year of secondary school and other schools whose diplomas give access to university studies (here, in the last year of secondary school, only those students in scientific sections and other sections with intensive mathematics programmes).

2. 1970-1971 survey (Comber and Keeves, 1973). Fourteen-year-old students and students in the final year of secondary school and in other institutions whose diplomas give access to university students.

3. Averages for all the countries covered by the survey, not merely those presented to the table. Mathematics, 13 years old, 10 countries; final year of secondary school in 8 countries. Science, 14 years old, 17 countries, final year in 15 countries.

4. At the time the surveys to which the table refers were carried out, nearly all children of age 13 or 14 in the countries considered were attending school, except in India (where only one quarter of 14-year-olds were in school). Depending on the education system in each country (as well as the definition adopted by the country for which schools give access to university studies or not), the proportion of students in the last year of high school compared to their total age group differs considerably, at the time of the surveys: in 1969, the Netherlands, 13%; India, 14%; England and Wales, 20%; Australia, 29%; Japan, 70%; the United States, 75% (according to Comber and Keeves, 1973).

of this extremely minute classification, the correlations range from 0.32 to 0.45 in rounded figures where basic general education subjects are concerned. The figures climb to 0.57 for English and 0.595 for knowledge of arts and literature.

Now let us consider the students. Table 9 is based on the studies of the IEA. The table represents pupils between 13 and 14 years of age and students in their last year at secondary school. Two subjects are concerned (mathematics and science) in six selected countries, one of which is a developing country. Four aspects of the social background and four aspects of kind of schooling were considered. The averages given in the last column concern all the countries involved in the studies in question (between eight and seventeen countries, depending on age group and subject), and not just the six countries shown in Table 9.

According to Table 9, the mean correlation category of social background/level for 13- and 14-year-old children is 0.24 with regard to mathematics and 0.23 with regard to science.

Five of the six countries listed in the table are developed countries. In these countries, the correlation ranges from 0.22 to 0.38. It is much lower for the sixth country, India. This value should not be interpreted as the effect of a greater degree of social homogeneity, quite the contrary. In the five developed countries, all children between 13 and 14 were attending school when the studies on which Table 9 is based were conducted. In India, this was only true of one-quarter of these children. In this country, consequently, the study involved a privileged minority within the total population. This minority tended to consist of individuals from relatively similar, affluent, backgrounds, as well as, probably, students of more humble origins, closely filtered out on the basis of scholastic performance. Under these conditions, the role of differences of social background is reduced.

For similar reasons, the correlation social class/level is generally very low in the last year of secondary school as well: on average, 0.08 for mathematics and 0.09 for science. The United States is an exception (0.24 and 0.21), because secondary school in that country ends with the last year of high school and, at the time, three-quarters of an age-group were already enrolled in high school.

The relationship between the other aspects of social background and the level of knowledge is less pronounced on the whole. It tends to differ similarly according to age group.

Let us now consider type of schooling, again referring to Table 9.

The correlation between level of the section (or school) attended and the level of knowledge of all members of an age group is naturally high when these individuals are split according to sections or schools which differ significantly in terms of their curricula, as well as the social background, aptitudes and motivation of the students attending these schools or sections. Accordingly, the value in this case was 0.74 for one of the countries in Table 9 at the time the studies were conducted. Obviously, the less an education system is partitioned in this way, the weaker is this correlation. The mean correlation between the type of section and the level of mathematical knowledge is 0.37 for 13-year-old students and 0.32 for those in their last year of high school, as shown in Table 9. The average correlations with regard to the type of school are low.

It does happen that one specific aspect of schooling conditions is quite clearly linked to such global differences as the type of section or school. In this case, the correlation tends to take on a certain significance. However, as a general rule, the real level of students is little influenced by any particular characteristic of a school, the curricula, methods, teaching staff, etc., taken separately. In this way, on the average, the correlation teachers/level of knowledge in Table 9 is virtually nil, with the exception of one country. Another example: the correlation number of hours per week/level of knowledge gravitates around zero, with a greater negative tendency than positive.

Explanatory impacts

As indicated in the preceding section, two-way classifications according to social background or kind of studies and the level of knowledge are the product of all influences combined, and these influences are the cause of two further kinds of differences of level: (a) differences of level within each social category when each category is broken down according to kind of school (within-group differences); (b) distribution differences between these categories according to level (between-group differences).

The analysis of the explanatory impacts divides total differences into two fractions: those which are within-group and those which are between-group.

The latter are considered to be explained - in the very relative sense of the statistical explanation, see below - by the social background or the kind of schooling. The former are on the contrary those which these variables do not explain. The calculations (see Chapter IV) proceed from correlations which summarize the two-way classifications.

They result in explanatory impacts (share of between-group differences) which at first are baffling because of their quantitative insignificance.

In such analyses, the variable corresponding to the differences to be explained is called the 'dependent variable'. Here the dependent variable is the inequality of knowledge. The variable or variables (differences) which produce the effect to be evaluated are called independent or, again, explanatory variables (social background, schooling in the present case).

The explanatory impacts are of two kinds: crude or partial. The crude impacts are those which are obtained when only one explanatory variable is taken into consideration. The partial impact is the result of a calculation involving two explanatory variables or more. Each is assigned its share of influence. The partial impacts differ to a lesser or greater extent depending on the method used for estimating them: direct impact, net impact or stepwise regression (see Chapter IV).

Here the notion of explanation is taken in the statistical sense of the word. It simply designates the relatively distinct relationships between the positions of individuals in their classifications. These classifications separate the members of a generation into categories, according to criteria related to the social background and kind of schooling being received or level of formal education attained. The same individuals are also divided into categories according to their level of knowledge.

The problem is to see to what extent classification from this point of view is a function of their classification according to one or more of the other criteria.

The expression 'explanatory variable' should not mislead. The members of one social category, like the elements of any statistical set obtained in other than strictly experimental conditions, are only similar from a single point of view, that of the classifying data item. The social background category is generally defined as the socio-professional group to which the father belongs. Fathers of members of the 'working class' social background category have occupations which statistical custom and the resultant statistical conventions assign to this vast socio-professional group. It is their only point in common. For the rest (income, family life-style, health status, personality type, education received, attitudes towards the education of their children, etc.), they represent extremely diverse cases. But, depending on the category, the mix of cases differs to varying degrees, which has repercussions, in particular, on the distribution of those surveyed according to their level of knowledge.

Table 10. Percentage crude and net explanatory impacts. Mathematics, students aged 13 years, 10 countries, 1964. Impacts (% of explained variance) and means[1]

	Crude explanatory impact	Net explanatory impact
A. *Variables having a net explanatory impact of at least 1% (five variables)*		
Section (primary, general, scientific, etc)	13.7	10.7
Student's degree of interest for mathematics	9.0	7.2
Father's socio-professional category	5.8	2.4
Time spent studying at home	3.6	1.5
Degree of similarity between problems covered in the classroom and test items	2.9	1.5
Subtotal (total explanatory impact of these five variables)		23.3
B. *Other variables included in the analysis (twenty variables)[2]*		
Mean impact of these variables	0.9	0.2
Subtotal (total explanatory impact of these twenty variables)		4.2
C. *Explanatory impact of all twenty-five variables*		27.5
Share of explained variance		72.5
Total		100%

1. Calculated according to data quoted by Husén et al. (1967). The table reads as follows: on average, in the ten countries to which these data refer, differences of section, in terms of their crude impact, explain 13.7% of the differences of level in mathematics, in the case of 13-year-old students. According to the multivariate analysis performed by the authors, the same variable (section), in terms of its net impact, explains on average 10.7% of the differences of level in mathematics, for the same 13-year-old students, etc. Since crude explanatory impacts partially overlap, they cannot be added. The ten countries are: Australia, Belgium, England and Wales, Finland, France, Japan, the Netherlands, Scotland, Sweden and the United States.
2. These twenty variables include, in particular: *family* (father's level of formal education; mother's formal level of education; locality of residence; whether or not the father has a scientific occupation); *teaching staff* (educational background of teaching staff, their salary, their degree of autonomy in the choice of curriculum and methods, number of hours of school per week, number of hours of mathematics per week, number of hours spent working at home per week, size of the school's student population, number of subjects, degree of individualisation of instruction according to the student's individual character, section, estimated expenditure per student in terms of teachers' salaries); *the student* (sex, age in months).

It is according to the extent these mixes differ that the explanatory impact of the social background category is measured. When the crude impact of a variable is determined, the cumulative effect of these differences are taken into consideration. Multivariate analysis (partial impacts) is based on the assumption that the individuals are separated into categories whose members resemble each other from two or more points of view (for example same social background category and same formal level of education). With twenty-five explanatory variables, as in Table 10, the number of categories can be very great (evaluating the impact of each of these variables would produce results analogous to those which would be obtained by grouping the individuals into categories whose members would be similar from the point of view of the twenty-four other factors). Nonetheless, this allows for a degree of heterogeneity of the members of a group, of these numerous subsets, but to a lesser extent than when fewer variables come into play. For example, one of the variables represented in Table 10 is the amount of expenditure per pupil, based on teachers' salaries.

The direct explanatory impact assigned to a variable does not consist in its strictly individual effect. It includes the effect of differences of attitude, subtle variations in the kind of education provided, etc., which still exist within the groups of students who are similar according to the twenty-four other explanatory categories. In particular, the inequality of expenditure per student no doubt varies rather markedly in certain countries, depending on family incomes (Coleman et al, 1966). Yet, this variable is not among those analysed in Table 10. Hence, however detailed they might be, the analyses contained in this table do not totally isolate the effect of any one variable. But they probably provide a rather close estimate of its effect.

The crude impact of a single explanatory variable is often as meaningful as its partial impact. This is true of the category 'social class'. It is the result of all of the influences related to the social class. In particular, it comprises in its entirety the degree of dependence between social background and level of knowledge attributable to the inequality of educational opportunity: children of working class origin have fewer opportunities than others, especially those of upper class origin, to prolong their studies (inequality with regard to education), which has repercussions, of course, on the inequality of level of knowledge according to social background.

Crude impacts say something about the 'all inclusive' incidence of a given aspect of differences of social condition, or of any other kind of differences. Multivariate analysis strives to dissociate the influences insofar as this is possible.

It should be emphasized that an explanatory impact indicates the relationship between differences: differences of social background or kind of school, on one hand, and on the other, differences in level of knowledge. It shows to what extent the latter are a function of the former. In other words, to what extent the inequality of social background or type of school can statistically explain the inequality of level of knowledge.

If social conditions differ little or, at least, the educative power of the milieu, the family in particular, differs little according to social category, the impact of social background tends to be very low. This does not mean that the background has little impact on the development of knowledge. It simply means that overall, its action is very similar, whatever the category of social background.

The same remark applies to the impact of schooling: a low impact means that educational efficiency varies little according to category of school attended by students, or the kind of school in which adults completed their education and the level achieved (formal level of education). When this impact is greater, this means that the efficiency of education differs more significantly from one category to the next. But it could just as well be small overall or qualitatively better.

Chapters III and IV develop these points in greater depth.

*   *   *

Work in experimental education or social psychology, the assessments of educational reforms and a number of other research efforts aim at a deeper explanation of the inequality of student performance, based on observations concerning the knowledge formation process or the level of knowledge at a given point in time, or again, more simply, on the basis of grades in school, amount of grade repeating, the breakdown of students by section at the crossroads of education systems. The publications which resulted can be numbered in thousands. Many make a very valuable contribution to the improvement of educational efficiency in the schools concerned. Some contribute to the fundamental knowledge of cognitive mechanisms. With regard to the effects of social background, curricula, school facilities and other school factors, they achieve various results, mostly contradictory. A given factor which, according to certain investigations, appears to have an extremely positive effect, has, according to others, a negative impact or none whatsoever. The probable reason for this is that in each particular situation, interactions between factors differ and that student achievement is a function of this network of relationships (Levine, Barnes et al., 1975; see also, various articles in the *International Encyclopedia of Education*).

The surveys which cover entire generations study the effect of all the situations in which knowledge development took place. They provide us with an overview.

*   *   *

Let us now look at the total explanatory impact of social background and education, in relation to the level of knowledge.

The total explanatory impact is calculated using the square of the correlation value expressing the degree of dependence between two variables, one of which (the independent or explanatory variable) is considered to affect the other (the dependent variable). Individuals are classified at different levels in terms of this dependent variable. The objective is to see to what extent these differences of level are the result of membership in groups which differ in terms of the explanatory variable (that is, to what extent these differences are between-group), or the effect of all other influencing factors taken as a whole (within-group differences). The square of a correlation expresses the ratio between-group differences/total differences (more precisely, in technical terms, it gives the fraction of explained variance). See Chapter IV.

A common correlation value, of between 0.1 and 0.4, corresponds to an explanatory impact of from 1 to 16%. A correlation of 0.5 - an exceptional value - corresponds to an explanatory impact of 25%. In this case, 75% of the differences present remain unexplained. These are between-group differences. Most often, the percentage of unexplained differences is between 85 and 95% or more.

This agrees with reality, as a glance at the two-way table will readily confirm. First, let us take Table 17 (page 100, social background and reading level, young men of 20 years, Switzerland). We ask ourselves whether the table reflects to some degree the order one would expect if a close correlation between background and level did exist. The more evident the order, the more the members of each background category will tend to fall into the same group in terms of level. In the extreme case - perfect order, a correlation of 1 - each social background category would have its specific level into which all of its members and only its members would fall. The social background category would determine the level, or, statistically speaking, would explain it.

However, what is most evident in this table is its lack of order. The individuals in each background category are extremely scattered in terms of levels. The category is of virtually no help in predicting the level.

Yet, patterns emerge from the percentages in Tables 18 and 20 nonetheless. The calculation of the explanatory impacts determines the share of each of them in the real distribution of cases. The ordered portion (between-group or 'explained' differences) is always smaller than the within-group share (unexplained differences).

In the real example given above, the correlation social background/knowledge level is 0.161. The corresponding crude explanatory impact (between-group differences) is 2.6%. The share due to between-group differences, those not explained, is thus 97.4% (Table 20, page 102).

The relationship formal level of education/level of knowledge allows less latitude for disorder (Tables 25 and 26) with regard to the same sample of young men. But disorder still predominates. In the present example, the formal level of education (correlation of 0.388) only explains 15.1% of the inequality of knowledge. The unexplained share is 84.5%. It is thus six times larger.

Table 10 concerns 13-year-old students in ten countries. The mean crude impact of social background is 5.8%. That of the section attended, the highest value recorded, is still only 13.7%.

The multivariate analysis method makes it possible to deal simultaneously with two or more variables (independent or explanatory variables) whose effects upon another variable (dependent variable) we wish to evaluate. We are no longer concerned with the crude impact of each explanatory variable, but rather, with its partial impact.

Multivariate analysis tends to reduce the share of each explanatory variable, while still increasing the share of total explained differences over the entire set of explanatory variables under consideration. The second column of Table 10 is the result of an analysis involving a particularly large number of explanatory variables, that is, twenty-five. Overall, the combined effect of all these variables explains around one-quarter of the inequality of knowledge. One of them, in terms of its net impact, explains 10.7% of this inequality. The variable concerned is the section attended. Social class in terms of net impact explains 2.4% of the inequality of knowledge. The majority of the selected variables taken individually have a minute effect. Twenty of the twenty-five taken altogether account for 4.2% of the differences of level. This gives each of them a mean partial explanatory impact of 0.2%. These twenty variables include the educational background of teachers, the number of hours of class per year, and other indicators related to the kind of schooling.

The relationship between inequality of opportunity and impacts

Although the inequality of achieving an acceptable general level of education depending on social background is great, this variable has only a minor impact on the inequality of knowledge. Likewise, although the differences of formal level of education have a significant influence on the probability of achieving this level, it only explains a fraction of the inequality of knowledge. The same applies to the effect on the knowledge of pupils of the kind of school being attended.

Chapter V explains in detail, using concrete examples, why this is true. This is very easy to grasp.

Let us suppose that 1% of the members of a socially or educationally disadvantaged class have a good, real level of education, whereas the proportion of individuals at the level from a privileged class is 50%. The latter have fifty times the chances of achieving this level.

Let us assume that each category comprises one-tenth of the population being considered. The comparison which has just been made in relation to the inequality of opportunity concerns only 5.1% of this total population, leaving out 94.9% of individuals. It could be that the distribution of the majority of the population is such as to suggest no dependence of the level of knowledge in relation to the other variable. As a result, the explanatory impact calculated globally may be small. This is what happens in reality. We need not be puzzled. Simply, we are dealing here with two genuine measurements, one of which is partial, the other, global.

Impacts and levels

It could well be that the impact of school variables, because of their magnitude, have little effect on the result of all of the influences involved. This, at least, is one question which the IEA surveys make it possible to raise. These studies are the only ones which allow us at present to place the question clearly. Indeed, dealing with this point requires international comparisons. Comparisons between regions with widely different education systems could also be helpful.

The IEA surveys show that, although the average level of pupils in the various subjects in the curriculum differs very significantly between Third World countries and industrialized countries, this level is quite comparable from one industrialized country to another.[2] One could jump to the conclusion that, in these countries, level depends little on possible differences in the breakdown of explanatory impacts in terms of social background, kind

Table II. *Structure of influences and overall result of their influence expressed as a percentage. Students 14 years old (1970-1971). Reading comprehension. Three industrialised countries*[1]

Country	Structure of influences (% of explained variance)					Results		
	Impact of social background, sex and age in months. 10 variables[2]	Impact of kind of schooling 16 variables[3]	Sub-total (26 variables)	Impact of other factors	Total	Mean level of knowledge (in points)[4]	Degree of inequality of knowledge[5]	Inequality of opportunity according to the social class of the parents[6]
New Zealand	13.5	25.8	39.3	60.7	100	29.3	11.0	0.27
Sweden	16.1	2.9	19.0	81.0	100	25.6	10.8	0.28
Netherlands	12.5	24.6	37.1	62.9	100	25.2	10.2	0.31

1. Thorndike (1973) and indications taken from Comber and Keeves (1973). New Zealand is the country in which the mean level of 14-year-old students was found to be the highest in this survey. Fifteen countries were involved. The Netherlands was the industrialised country in which the mean level was lowest. Sweden is the country in which the explanatory impact of kind of schooling was least significant. This concerns the total explanatory impact of each group of variables according to multivariate analysis (stepwise regression).

2. Socio-professional category of the father, his formal level of education, mother's education, number of books in the family library, the presence of dictionaries, their utilisation by members of the family, newspapers, magazines. Number of children. Sex and age in months of the student.

3. Type of school: New Zealand (girls', boys', or co-ed schools); Sweden (two categories of schools, of not very significant dissimilarity); the Netherlands (five categories, from trade schools to high schools with sections subject to selective enrolment). As well as the student's level, the number of hours of instruction per week, the number of hours per week spent on homework, number of students per class, the degree of specialisation of teachers, in particular, those teaching the mother tongue.

4. Mean score in points of all students of 14 years of age.

5. Standard deviation. The greater this value is, the less clustering around the mean value, hence, the greater the inequality among students with regard to their level in reading comprehension.

6. Correlation between score and social class (defined by the socio-professional category of the father and his formal level of education).

of schooling, and other factors. Inspection of the data shows that such differences do exist.

Table 11 concerns three industrialized countries (New Zealand, Sweden, the Netherlands). It shows the reading comprehension abilities of 14-year-olds. The table is divided into two parts: (a) structures of influences; (b) outcomes of the action of all the influences present.

In this table, the structure of influences is organized into three blocks:

1. *Impact of social background,* defined here by eight variables: this block contains two further variables, sex and exact age in months. The impact of this first block is thus that of all the influences whose effects vary more or less absolutely with variations in eight aspects of the family's social background, together with the variables sex and exact age (exactly 14 years or just going on 15).

2. *Kind of schooling.* Involved here is the global impact of all the influences - independent of those in block 1 - whose effects vary more or less absolutely with variations in differences related to the educational framework.

3. *Other influences.* All those which are independent of the influences in blocks 1 and 2.

In the right-hand part of the table, the effects of the action of all the factors involved are presented according to three different points of view: (a) the generation's mean reading comprehension level; (b) degree of scattering of individual levels around this mean (inequality of individual knowledge); (c) degree of inequality of opportunity (to attain a good level of reading comprehension rather than to score low) according to parental social status, defined by the father's socio-professional category and formal level of education.

New Zealand is included in this table because it is the country in which the mean level of 14-year-old students happened to be the highest according to the survey. The Netherlands is the industrialized country in which the mean was lowest. The distance with respect to New Zealand, however, is not great. Sweden is the country where the impact of kind of schooling was the least.

With regard to the results, these three countries are very close to each other. New Zealand leads only a little with regard to the mean level. The degree of inequality of intellectual levels is very similar for these three countries, just as is the degree of inequality of opportunity.

Thus, in these three societies, the habits, mentalities, social structures, economic conditions, media, educational set-up and all the other factors on which the level of 14-year-olds in the subject being compared depends, had roughly the same outcome.

But the channelling of these influences was very different in one country in comparison to the other two.

In New Zealand and the Netherlands, the situation in this respect was very similar. Differences of social background - as defined here, that is, very precisely - explain around 13% of the inequality of knowledge in question; differences in kind of schooling - also extremely precise - around 25%. Overall, the impact of social background and that of kind of schooling explain 39.3% of the inequality of knowledge in New Zealand and 37.1% in the Netherlands.

In Sweden, the total impact of these two categories of variables is only 19.0%, that is, one half as much. This is due to the fact that, in this country, the impact of the kind of schooling was negligible (2.9%). The determinants of the differences acted via other channels: via social background to a slightly greater extent than in the two other countries (impact of 16.1%); and especially to a much greater extent via influences from the third block, those which are independent both of social class and school factors.

In the three countries, it is the weight of influences of this kind which is most significant. They explain around two-thirds of the inequality of knowledge in New Zealand and the Netherlands. In Sweden: over 80%.

In New Zealand and the Netherlands, the inequality of knowledge to which Table 11 refers is three-quarters dependent on factors other than the educational set-up. In Sweden, these non-school related factors account for 97% of the inequality of knowledge.

These examples suggest that overall, given an analogous cultural context, the sum total of interactions taking place over the years have about the same effect on a generation, regardless of the educational set-up. Even in cases where the educational set-up plays a comparatively significant role, the remaining factors are several times more powerful.

*　　　*　　　*

In Sweden, the schools attended by 14-year-old students differed very little. The kind of schooling was more of a constant (all students were roughly equal in this regard) than a variable. In these circumstances it is normal that the explanatory impact of the kind of schooling, because it is a measurement of effects of differences, should be nearly zero. The determinants of inequality of knowledge nonetheless played their part. This is because, in

Sweden as elsewhere, despite the great similarity between schools, there were students who differed considerably with respect to individual characteristics and milieu. The great homogeneity of the Swedish school system seems not to have attenuated the effects of non-school differences.

In the Netherlands and New Zealand, schools and sections differed to a greater extent. The distribution of students according to individual characteristics and the exact type of social background, affective context within the family, etc., also differed to a certain degree between schools and sections in these countries. A part of the impact of these non-school related differences is attributed to the kind of schooling. This involves the differences of social background which are independent of the variables used to define social background in the model used here.

The fact that the impact of kind of school was greater in these countries than in Sweden obviously does not imply that education in Sweden is less effective. The efficiency of an education system as a whole, and the comparative efficiency of categories of schools and sections of which it is made up are two different things. Analysis of the explanatory impact of schooling envisages the situation from the second standpoint.

In New Zealand and the Netherlands, for reasons both school-related (differences between programmes, equipment, etc.) and non-school related (differences from the point of view of individual characteristics and of background, not covered by the survey), the efficiency of various categories of schools (or sections) proved to be quite different. In Sweden, the efficiency of all of them was roughly the same at the time of the survey, in the subject concerned.

The instructional means were distributed differently, and the students as well. All things considered, the result was roughly the same. Here, very powerful sociological forces seem to have produced an equal distribution of knowledge despite the particularities of each country's education system.

The fact that in countries which are profoundly alike in their ways of thinking, living and production, the global result of millions of events affecting individual destinies is similar, despite differences which characterize these countries on the surface - in particular, from the point of view of aspects dependent on political decisions - is not only restricted to the field of effective teaching. It is also the case in many others fields. Examples which come to mind are demographic data such as birth rates, or life expectancies.

Conclusions

The preceding comments summarize rather well what this and the previous chapter attempt to make clear, namely that the extra-scholastic context is the main determinant of the degree of dissemination of general education. We have seen this from several points of view:

(a) The degree to which young people's level in the various subjects depends on the evolution of the education system (Chapter I) is very low. The education system is developing rapidly. Yet levels are declining. The decline appears to affect the core subjects of compulsory education. In others, on the contrary, there has been improvement. Apparently these subjects correspond to needs which are in demand for modern life (English as a foreign language, computer science).

(b) The massive predominance of extra-scholastic factors in the explanation of the inequality of knowledge, based on crude impacts and impacts revealed by multivariate analyses.

(c) Similar general level of students in industrialized countries for which IEA data are available. Similarity also between the observations made in the United States and Switzerland with regard to the level of young adults. A very different overall level operates in Third World countries.

(d) Hence, there is no apparent effect on the level of general education in industrialized countries caused by differences in the organization of education systems. The examples given in Table 11 confirm this.

The fact that differences in social background result in a significant degree of inequality of opportunity in terms of access to effective education, that the gaps in this regard are extremely great depending on the level of formal education or the kind of studies being pursued, if the educational institutions attended by students are non-uniform, does not contradict what has just been said. We have seen why.

Taken separately, individual aspects of the nature of the curricula, methods and equipment of schools, and the educational background of teachers has only a slight influence on the level of knowledge. This is not surprising. All other things being equal, there is no reason why the amount of money spent per pupil, the specific methods used, the number of pupils per class, etc., should necessarily lead, on the average, to a measurable difference in the performance of pupils, especially when they have only been attending the schools in question for a short time.

This is not to say that education has no impact. It would certainly be absurd to make such an assertion. What is true, is that it plays a role within a given social context in which a whole set of other influences affect the evolution of individual knowledge, before, during and after attending school. Overall, the combination of these influences is far more powerful than the influence exerted by schools.

These influences act upon the initial acquisition of knowledge by the individual and the later expansion of such knowledge, through the motivations and opportunities for reinforcement they provide (frequency of utilization of knowledge, for practical reasons or out of curiosity or personal priorities). The extra-scholastic context stimulates interest (motivation) in certain forms of knowledge, and favours their frequent utilization. It has the inverse effect in other areas.

In economic terms, one could speak of a demand for certain forms of knowledge to designate the degree to which the total of these manifestations is useful to individuals: every individual either feels much, little or no need for a given form of knowledge at a given point in time (motivation); each individual often, seldom or never needs a given kind of knowledge for work, leisure, or whatever other reason.

Demand is a function of the condition of society. It is not the same in an age of mysticism as in an age of materialism (Sorokin, 1957, 1962, 1964). It is not the same in developing countries as in industrialized countries. It varies according to age, social milieu, profession, and many other parameters.

One can also speak of a supply of knowledge. It consists of all the information and stimuli for learning which are in circulation. They are first transmitted through informal contacts of all types which take place in the family, the neighbourhood, the school, the business, etc. To this is added the deluge of information arising from all agents explicitly interested in informing, training, persuading, inciting to reflection, arousing emotions, entertaining - in short, influencing minds. They rely upon the spoken word, books and the media, in particular. Education is one of these agents.

The supply of knowledge in our day and age is enormous. Individuals are literally bombarded with sounds, words and pictures. If what is being communicated to them in this way is to do more than merely flash across their field of perception, they must take an interest in it, in other words, there must exist a link between the supply and the demand.

Making a pupil absorb knowledge to which he feels little affinity or which he will have few opportunities to put into practice is an arduous task and the results are often disheartening. The classics in educational science have always insisted on this point (see in particular Claparede, 1921).

This is to say that to bring the entire population beyond the level of effective demand for knowledge is an extremely difficult undertaking.

In subjects where the demand is falling, the level falls, whatever effort schools might make. This does not mean that the schools are ineffective. They must contend with contradictory forces which reduce the immediate results of their efforts (the progress of pupils) and tend to lessen these results even more further downstream (lack of recall by adults). In subjects where the demand is growing, the immediate and long-term results are better.

The decisive factor in the psychological process upon which the individual level of knowledge depends, is apparently its degree of usefulness, as perceived by children and adolescents, and, later on, by adults. The degree of usefulness is in turn a function of the complexion of the cultural context.

Like a yacht, education must steer its course, making the most skilful use of the favourable winds that blow. Against adverse winds, its only recourse is to sail close-hauled, laboriously.

Notes

1. The Coleman Report sparked numerous scientific, educational and political debates in the United States and in other countries. But its audience in some regions of the world was sometimes limited to only a handful of specialists. Cherkaoui commented that in France, from 1966, the year this study was published, until 1979 the report had only been quoted in two works, whereas elsewhere the books and articles which refer to it number in the hundreds (Cherkaoui, 1979). The same can be said with regard to IEA surveys and other similar studies.

2. Chile, India and Iran took part in the IEA surveys on reading comprehension and basic science knowledge. The mean score in reading comprehension for pupils of 14 years ranges from 5 to 14 points in these countries. Again, this concerns only school-going pupils. If all other 14-year-olds were included, the mean would obviously drop. In this subject, at 14, the mean score in industrialized countries ranges from 25 to 29 points (Thorndike, 1973). Basic science, likewise at age 14: in Chile, India and Iran from 6 to 9 points; industrialized countries; between 21 and 31 points (Comber & Keeves, 1973).

CHAPTER THREE

Factors affecting the inequality of knowledge

However banal it might be to say so, the mind is not some malleable substance upon which schools and other institutions print lasting knowledge at will, with a finished product which in terms of quality and quantity corresponds exactly to the means invested. An individual's knowledge in no matter what area is the product of an entire set of - interdependent - factors. Let us look at three examples.

First, Peter and Paul who are about to sit their A-levels. Peter is sickly, timid. At each oral exam he is frightened to death. Nothing comes easily to him. Nonetheless he managed to reach the last year of secondary school, for he always worked hard and his teachers often gave him a helping hand because of his handicaps and, to some extent, because his father is deceased and his mother, a very active member of parent/teacher association, works very hard in a factory.

Paul is one of the best players on the junior football team. He would like to do a degree in literature. One of his English and Latin teachers contributed a great deal to instilling in him a fondness for reading. What is more, two or three of his close friends also intend to study literature. But Paul is hopeless in trigonometry. The teacher, it must be said, is deplorable. Paul also has very poor marks in science. The lessons for this subject take place at the same time his girlfriend has a court for one hour at the tennis club. He often preferred tennis with her to natural science. Two months before exams, he crammed in 'trig' and 'sci'. His father, a lawyer, is not at all keen on seeing him fail and pays for private lessons.

All goes well for Peter and Paul. They successfully pass their A-levels. Twenty years later neither of them has retained the slightest notion of trigonometry. They hardly remember more than a few words of Latin.

Peter became the employee of a tax adviser, after having failed his law degree. Outside the office, he spends his time in front of the television.

His younger brother, John, our third example, never liked school. Unlike his older brother, he was always full of confidence. He left school at age 15 and became a garage mechanic. The active member of a political party, he writes well-informed, penetrating articles.

Paul only studied literature for two years. He married young, had children very early, and took the first job offer that came. Later on, his company sent him to California. There, after changing companies several times, he become a very prosperous software salesman. He reads a great deal, in particular, works on the history of music. Few experts would challenge him in this subject.

*   *   *

How, in such cases, as in any individual case, can we unravel the respective contributions of curricula, teachers, friends, personality, social class, and a thousand other influences? Together they form a tangled succession of circumstances, leading to a certain level for a given individual, in a given field, at a given time.

At a numerically more significant scale, statistics show that certain factors have a greater impact than others in an average number of cases. However, since in reality no one factor alone exerts a decisive influence - if we set aside cases of severe mental impairment - the share of each in the explanation of the inequality of knowledge is always extremely small. The share of most of them is even infinitesimal.

What is more, a factors's share of influence is never really isolated, as we shall see. But let us first review the kinds of factors involved.

Overview of the factors influencing the inequality of knowledge

The abilities demonstrated by an individual at a given time in a given subject depends on interaction between two types of factors: personal and contextual. The former correspond to all the individual characteristics which had an influence on the evolution of these skills in the past and also have an influence on their manifestation in the present. The latter correspond to all the related characteristics, both physical and social, which have affected this

Figure 4. *Factors which determine individual levels of knowledge*

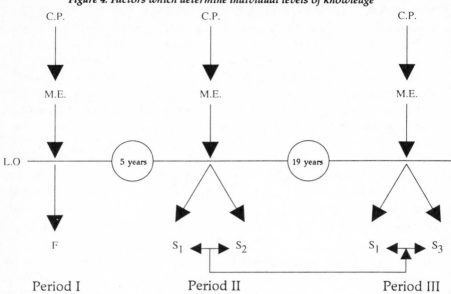

evolution in the past and act upon the manifestation of knowledge in the present.

Personal factors

Figure 4 gives an average individual case. It treats ten personal factors separately. Many others could, of course, intervene. Examples of these other personal factors will be given later on.

The personal factors considered separately are:

1. *Age.* The diagram is divided into three parts: I. the pre-school period; II. the period between enrolment in school and late adolescence; III. the period, much longer than the others, corresponding to the entire span of adult life.

2/3. *The mental processes of learning (L) and of oblivescence (O).* Learning (in the psychological sense of the word) is the increase of the amount of information stored in the memory, of the ability to assimilate new information instantly through the perception of objects and situations, as well as through written texts, pictures and documents of all kinds. More importantly, it is also the increased capacity to sort this information and to use reasoning to co-ordinate and transform it into acts in the form of some external manifestation (movements, words, actions on matter, utilization of tools, machines, etc.) or an internal occurrence (becoming aware of a fact, reflecting, etc. for oneself, nothing more). Oblivescence or forgetting is the opposite: it is unlearning. These faculties are two facets of one psychological process. This is a lifelong process (Piaget, 1973).

4-8. *These are the manifestations of the level which this process has enabled the individual to achieve at a given point in time.* The abilities which the individual demonstrated at a given time, for example, in a game, in a school exam, during a test, at work.

In Figure 4, with respect to the pre-school period, these manifestations are designated by the letter F. This refers to the sum total of the manifestations of the basic knowledge acquired at a very young age, ranging from the fundamentals of logic and the bulk of the concepts, expressions and intonations which make up language, to many other kinds of knowledge.

With regard to the period which follows, two unspecified kinds of knowledge are designated by S_1 and S_2. For example, these could involve the results of a test in composition, geography or any other subject in the curriculum. This could also concern activities of a practical nature or the score obtained on a test which is part of a survey.

During period III in Figure 4, that is, at some point during the individual's adult life, his abilities in one of the subjects (S_1) considered during Period II will again be evaluated. In addition, the individual's abilities in another field could be taken into account, for example, his professional skills (S_3).

The manifestations of knowledge only partially reflect, depending on circumstances, the latent potential (the status of the L/O process at the time of the observation) of an individual's knowledge. For example, the individual could take a very serious attitude towards a test and work very hard, or take it lightly. We would like to evaluate the latent potential, but must content ourselves with manifestations which only give an approximation of it.

9. *Motivation (M).* This is the desire to learn specific kinds of knowledge S_1 - S_3. The sources of such motivation are diverse. They range from spontaneous curiosity, whether superficial and transient, or more profound and permanent, to fear of not obtaining a good grade, of displeas-

ing parents, to imperatives of a professional nature, etc. Motivation is
the major catalyst of learning.

10. *Exercise (E)*. The frequency of utilization of a given kind of knowledge:
at home, for recreation, at school; later on, at work, in the exercise of
political responsibilities, etc. The greater the frequency, the less impact
oblivescence (O) will have and, in turn, the more learning (L) will tend
to increase knowledge.

Other personal factors

Physical state (including cerebral); psychological equilibrium; personality;
age; sex; rank in the family (eldest, youngest, in-between); qualifications;
occupation; professional grade level; work schedule and vacation time;
nationality (in a given country: native, immigrant worker, etc.); forms of
recreation; integration versus fringe status, drugs; future plans; etc.

All these personal factors other than those classified under 1 to 10 are
represented by P. They act, or are capable of, acting upon motivation (M)
and on exercise (E), and consequently on learning and oblivescence (L/O)
and ultimately on the knowledge retained (F, S_1, S_2 and S_3).

Contextual factors (background)

In Figure 4 these are designated by C. This category concerns all the factors
which cause variations in the physical environment (climate, landscape, for
example) or social environment with which the individual is in contact.
They vary depending on the country, social category, occupation, business,
family, network of relationships, the kind of school attended, etc. In an
identical physical and social framework, they may vary according to individual behaviour. But this comes under the heading of the effects of personal
factors.

The components of the social universe are social relationships, both on
a large and a small scale, in their political, economic, educational, family
and other aspects, together with all the constraints which they entail, all the
stimuli they provide, all the advantages they afford, all the possibilities they
create, all the ideas they convey and inspire, from the most humble and
familiar to the most complex, all the desires and emotions they arouse.

These are the effects of the social context which the analysis of the
influence of social factors attempts to detect. Above and beyond comparisons between countries, these include classifications according to, inter alia,
social class, current school attended or education completed.

Identifying the different factors

The differentiation between influences begins with the breaking down of a population into classes whose members are similar in one respect or in more than one respect. Otherwise, they differ, but in general not as significantly as compared with the overall sample population. These classes therefore constitute strata in a statistical sense: subsets, the composition of which, from many points of view, tends to differ systematically, to lesser or greater degrees, compared with the composition in other sub-groups of the total set and with the total set itself.

Table 12. Example of factoring: an election poll (percentages)

	Votes cast		
	For A	For B	Total
Men	43	57	100
Women	45	55	100
Persons aged 18-34	35	65	100
Persons over 34	48	52	100
Blue-collar workers	36	64	100
Other social groups	48	52	100
Average	44	56	100

The most commonly known case is no doubt that of the categories according to which the results of opinion polls are presented. Let us analyse the way votes are cast (see Table 12) in an election for two candidates, A and B. Let us suppose that, as is often done, voters are grouped according to sex, age and social class. We can imagine the following distribution.

In each stratum, votes are cast for one or the other of the two candidates, but not in the same proportion. In each individual case, a large number of factors came into play. They will have affected the acquisition and development of the subject's political opinions, as well as, at that particular time, his/her vote. The collective result (percentage of votes for A and B) of the action of all of these factors differs according to the stratum.

In this example we are confronted with the determinants of choice, rather than with those of level of knowledge.

The factoring out of the influences determining the real level of knowledge begins with simple two-way tables comparing levels according to country, social class, current type of schooling, formal level of education, for example.

Let us take Tables 17 and 24 (pages 100 and 104). They concern the real level of a generation of young men in a subject, according to their social background: working class, middle class or upper class.

Each of these categories is a stratum, in which incomes, lifestyles, aspirations, attitudes towards school, and many other individual and contextual characteristics differ. But, in each stratum, the breakdown of cases according to income bracket, kinds of lifestyle, etc., is more or less individual. What these tables show is the effect of these differences on the composition of the mix of these individual cases on the classification of young men according to their level in the subject being considered.

In each individual case, a number of personal and contextual factors played a part: standard of living and lifestyle, health, motivation, amount of exercise, curricula, friends, parental attitudes, etc.

These factors influence the psychological processes of learning and of forgetting, and, ultimately, some of them influence in extremis the manifestations of knowledge reported by the survey. Altogether, in each of the three strata, nearly all imaginable factors probably played some kind of role. But the overall effect of these factors, the distribution of the members of each social category according to level of knowledge is not the same. The mean level of knowledge differs according to social category as well.

The distribution of pupils according to the kind of schooling they are currently receiving, or of adults according to their formal level of education also defines strata within which all the individual factors and co-factors - the same total number - exert their influences. The resultant distribution according to level of knowledge differs more or less from one stratum to the other.

Multivariate analysis introduces strata whose members are similar according to more than just one or even two criteria. For example, in a multivariate analysis involving the direct effects (see Chapter IV) of social category and those of the formal level of education, two series of strata are taken into consideration.

Let us suppose that there are three social categories (S_1, S_2 and S_3), three formal levels of education (L_1, L_2 and L_3), and three levels of knowledge (K_1, K_2 and K_3). The exercise consists then, as illustrated by Table 13, in

Table 13. Example. Strata conditioning the multivariate analysis of the influence of two different variables.

First phase			Second phase		
L_1S_1	L_2S_1	L_3S_1	S_1L_1	S_2L_1	S_3L_1
L_1S_2	L_2S_2	L_3S_2	S_1L_2	S_2L_2	S_3L_2
L_1S_3	L_2S_3	L_3S_3	S_1L_3	S_2L_3	S_3L_3

estimating the degree to which levels differ in nine strata from two points of view.

From the first point of view, the portion due to differences in social background is identified, controlling for the level of education. From the second point of view, the same is done with respect to the portion due to differences in formal level of education, controlling for the social background.

These two fractions, namely that attributed to social background and that attributed to the formal level of education, do not correspond to the total influence on the level of knowledge exerted by all factors involved. These factors have in this respect a share of influence - which is by far the main one - independently of their more or less systematic linkage to both social background and formal level of education.

Thus, the same factors are always involved. In the present example, multivariate analysis differentiates three of them: that of social background (and everything which goes with it); formal level of education (and everything which goes with it); and the rest, that is, the share of influences which depend neither on social background nor on formal level of education.

When an analysis attempts to estimate the share of more than two variables, the same principle is applied. The greater the number of variables, the smaller the share of each specific variable will be (the same applies to the 'remainder', the share of those influences not related to the variables whose effects are being measured).

An analysis which attempts, for example, to estimate the proportional direct effect of twenty variables would indicate the portion accounted for by each one of them, controlling for the other variables. This would be equivalent to supposing that the population were divided up into a large number of strata. For example, if the number of hours of class per year in the last school attended was one of the twenty variables, these strata would be composed of similar individuals according to their classification on the basis of nineteen variables and would only differ according to the number of hours of class per year at the end of their schooling. No doubt these strata would be quite homogenous from many points of view. One would be considerably closer to an evaluation of the effect due exclusively (that is, all other things being equal) to differences in the number of hours of class.

In general, analyses of this type which have been carried out produce very small or zero shares. This is not at all surprising. The factors involved in the level of knowledge are extremely numerous. They exert their influence over the years in combinations varying according to individuals and circumstances. Their effect is not always exerted in the same direction and with the same intensity. Not one of these factors in itself can therefore explain, for the average number of cases, more than a small fraction of the differences in question. It could happen that a factor for which a survey has been singled out may prove to have no effect whatsoever on a given kind of knowledge.

It should be added that, often, the action of one variable occurs over a rather short period of time. For example, if the observation concerns pupils of 14, having, until age 13, attended primary schools whose curricula differ slightly, it is quite comprehensible that this cannot have a great impact on their basic level of knowledge.

The same applies to, for example, differences in the formal level of education according to the kind of training provided to 15 to 18 or 20 year olds after compulsory school attendance. This three-to-four year interval is certainly very important. But is preceded by fifteen other years which are no less important, quite the contrary.

Impacts and efficiency

To avoid misunderstandings, let us emphasize that the explanatory impacts to which the factoring of influences leads must not be taken for measurements of the power of, for example, the educative action of the family or the school.

In a country in which differences of social class, measured according to the status of the parents, have very little relation to differences in the level of knowledge (hence, a very low explanatory impact), it is entirely probable that, in general, the family be nonetheless a powerful vector of individual knowledge development. It is because, overall, the influence exerted within the various social categories is very similar, that the explanatory impact of social background is negligible.

The explanatory impact of schooling indicates the extent to which the differences of levels of knowledge correspond to differences between schools (for the sake of brevity, we will use this expression to mean all school-related differences: section, curricula, methods, formal level of education, etc.). It involves the relation between the educational selection process (distribution by kinds of school) and division of knowledge (grouping according to level of knowledge). The question is analogous to those related to the choice of school and adult social status, choice of school and adult income, etc.

In a country in which all compulsory schools were very similar, both with regard to the nature and the quality of instruction, which is quite often almost the case, the explanatory impact of compulsory education on the level of knowledge would tend to be zero, if the differences within the pupil sample in terms of motivation, social background, and so on were also controlled. This would, of course, not imply that educational efficiency was abysmal. It could just as well be average or high.

Rather, efficiency would practically not differ at all according to the category of school (large, small, rural, urban, for example).

Impact analysis does not tell us whether individuals learn more at school or outside it. But it does indicate to what extent the inequality of given forms of knowledge depends on differences in social condition, kinds of schooling being received or already completed, etc. The answers to these questions are certainly not without interest.

Other observations are necessary, for example, on the subject of the sources (school, home environment, work, media, etc.) of various forms of knowledge or of the extent and causes of the gap between real knowledge levels and desired levels.

CHAPTER FOUR

An analysis of explanatory impacts

The formulas which will be used in the calculations below can be found in manuals of statistics and computer science (cf. Boudon, 1967, 1971, 1982; Blalock, 1972; Wright, 1979; Asher, 1976; Van de Geer, 1971; Nie et al. 1975). They will not be reproduced here. In practice, these very long calculations are not done manually. Computers do the work with the help of ready-made programmes.

Our objective will simply be to explain, in the most easily comprehensible language possible, the nature of these operations and the significance of the results they give. When examples are required, we will refer to the data contained in the Annex to Chapters II to V (pages 99 to 109). All of them are drawn from the 1984 Swiss survey concerning the level of knowledge of young adults (males).

Computing the explanatory impacts[1] consists in separating the differences into two parts: explained differences (those which depend on the factor or factors of which we wish to evaluate the effect) and unexplained differences (the remaining ones).

'Explain' is taken here in the purely statistical sense of a quantitative relation within the limitations of the kind of calculations made. The pinpointing of the real causes of the relationships thus revealed is a question of verifying hypotheses via ad hoc observations.

The variables whose effects are to be evaluated here will be social background and formal level of education. We take as given that they affect knowledge. We will restrict ourselves to knowledge acquired through general education.

Statistically speaking, this is equivalent to determining the extent to which the classification (or differences) by social background and the classi-

fication (differences) by formal level of education coincide with the classification (differences) according to the level in various general education
subjects.

Crude impacts

Let us begin with a two-variable case only: an 'independent' or 'explanatory'
variable (whose effect is to be measured) and a 'dependent' variable (which
undergoes the effect which is to be measured). For example, social background (explanatory variable) and reading level (dependent variable).
Table 17 (Annex to Chapters II to V, page 100) shows in absolute numbers
the distribution according to these two variables of a sample representing a
generation of young men (Switzerland, 1984) from the survey just mentioned.

The analysis of these two variables is very important. It brings out the
total influence (crude explanatory impact) of all the factors which are not
completely independent of the explanatory variable. The crude impact of
social background - as defined in Table 16: working class, middle class,
upper class - thus includes the influence of differences in income, language,
aspirations, etc. which are tied, closely or remotely, to class differences. The
crude impact of this variable includes, in particular, the effects of inequality
of opportunity according to social background in terms of the scholastic
survival rate: the chance of extending one's studies over a lengthy period of
time rather than a short period of time differs according to social class, which
in turn has repercussions on the real level of general education. In other
words, when we say 'explanatory impact of social background' we include
everything which goes with it. The same applies to the impact assigned to
any other variable, as was pointed out in Chapter III.

Let us take a look at two approaches in estimating the crude explanatory
impact: using the eta^2 coefficient and the square coefficient of linear correlation.

The eta^2 coefficient

Calculating the eta^2 coefficient is useful when the dependent variable is
metric and the other non-metric. Metric: the levels of the variable are based
on measurements and are expressed by numbers, hence, the distances
between them are known. Examples: age, income, number of rooms in a
dwelling, number of test exercises successfully completed, etc. Non-metric:
nominal variable, the categories are simply distinct (sex, religion, etc.);
ordinal variables, the categories are ranked hierarchically, but the intervals

between them is not determined (primary schooling, apprenticeship papers, university degree, labourer, skilled worker, foreman, etc.). With the help of a justifiable measure of sleight of hand, ordinal variables can be made approximately metric for the needs of certain analyses. Nominal variables can also be adapted to the requirements of metric analyses.

Calculations related to the eta^2 coefficient do not entail such transformations. Let us take a case involving an explanatory (non-metric) variable and a dependent variable (metric). Each member of the population concerned ($\underline{P}$) is classified both according to the explanatory variable ($\underline{X}$) and the dependent variable ($\underline{Y}$). The eta^2 coefficient is determined as a means of evaluating the effect of the first on the second.

If $\underline{X}$ had no effect on $\underline{Y}$, the distribution of cases in $\underline{Y}$ would tend (consideration must be given to the probability of factors producing small random differences) to be identical for all categories of $\underline{X}$, hence, the same as for the entire population ($\underline{P}$) as well. The same would be true of the mean value of $\underline{Y}$. This is the so-called null hypothesis. It is illustrated in Figure 5.

Figure 5. Independence of two variables. Null hypothesis. Hypothetical example.

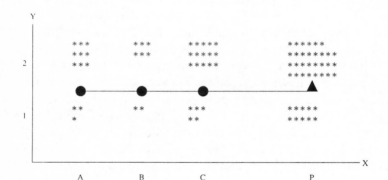

* = an individual

X = explanatory variable. Three non-metric categories: A, 12 individuals; B, 8; C, 20.

Y = level in a given area. Two levels: 1, one point (10 individuals); or 2, two points (30 individuals).

● = mean Y score of the members of each category A - C.

▲ = mean Y score over P.

Table 14. Independence of two variables. Null hypothesis. Figure 5 in figures.

Category (X)	Level (Y)		Total
	1	2	
In absolute numbers			
A	3	9	12
B	2	6	8
C	5	15	20
Total population (P)	10	30	40

Category (X)	Level (Y)		Total
	1	2	
In % (points of arrival - level - with category in (X) as point of departure)			
A	25	75	100
B	25	75	100
C	25	75	100
Total population (P)	25	75	100

Category (X)	Level (Y)		Total
	1	2	
In % (recruitment - according to explanatory variable - from each level)			
A	30	30	30
B	20	20	20
C	50	50	50
Total population (P)	100	100	100

Category (X)	Average level (Y)[1]
Average levels (Y) in points	
A	1.75
B	1.75
C	1.75
Total population (P)	1.75

1. For example, for category A: 3 cases of degree 1 = 3; 9 cases of degree 2 = 18. A total of 12 cases (3 + 18 = 21/12 = 1.75)

Table 14 shows what the hypothetical example of Figure 5 gives in terms of absolute figures, percentages, and mean scores.

In the hypothetical example, the explanatory variable ($\underline{X}$) consists of three categories (A, B, C) and the dependent variable, two levels (1 and 2 points). In the three categories and, thus, in the total sample, the distribution by level is proportionally the same. Conversely, at each level, and hence for the entire population, the distribution by category is the same. The mean score is the same in the three categories A, B, and C and in the total population $\underline{P}$. The explanatory impact of $\underline{X}$ is nil.

This, of course, does not imply that there are no differences between individuals from the point of view of $\underline{Y}$ (except in the extreme case in which all individuals would be at the same level in $\underline{Y}$).

In Figure 5, some are at level 1 and others at 2. Simply, these differences have nothing to do with the fact of being classified in categories A, B, or C.

The greater the gap between this and the real situation, the greater the effect of the explanatory variable. This is what the eta^2 coefficient measures.

To calculate this coefficient, the differences in $\underline{Y}$ are expressed in terms of variance. Variance is the mean (square) deviation of the positions of the members of a group about the overall mean.

Three kinds of variance are possible:

$\underline{V}$ = *Total variance.* Calculated according to the dispersion in $\underline{Y}$ of the population $\underline{P}$ taken individually, around the mean of all $\underline{Y}$ values. The $\underline{X}$ variable is not taken into consideration. Let us take our real example, that of the relationship between category of social background and reading level (see Annex). In this example, the overall mean of $\underline{Y}$ values is 1.896 points (Table 25). In this case, $\underline{V}$ is calculated relative to this mean.

$\underline{V}_{within}$ = *Within-group variance.* Also calculated in terms of the dispersion of the members of a population $\underline{P}$ taken individually, but in comparison with the mean of all $\underline{Y}$ values specific to their rank in $\underline{X}$. In our real example, for the 265 UC (upper-class members) dispersed around 2.272 points, for the 1176 MC (middle-class members), compared to 1.901 points and for the 739 WC (working-class members), compared with 1.754 points.

$\underline{V}_{between}$ = *Between-group variance.* Calculated considering each category of $\underline{X}$ as a unit: dispersion of these units according to their mean in $\underline{Y}$ dispersed around the overall mean of $\underline{P}$ in $\underline{Y}$. In our real example: for the 265 UC, 2.272; for the 1176 MC, 1.901; for the 739 WC, 1.734 over, in the three cases, 1.896.

*   *   *

The within-group variance is termed 'unexplained'. This means that it is not the result of membership in one or the other categories of $\underline{X}$: more precisely, it is not the result of the influence of all factors tied to $\underline{X}$.

It is the product of other influences which are independent of $\underline{X}$. Some of these influences tend to place individuals above the mean of their class by a little or by a lot (positive factors) and others (negative factors) have the inverse effect. In our real example, these factors disperse the UC's around the mean level (2.272 points) of their class. These factors have the same effect in the two other social categories, around their respective means.

But it is because such influences are present that the variable $\underline{X}$ (here, social background) has no impact. Depending on the categories of $\underline{X}$, the result of the negative and positive effects of the action of all the factors at work, independent or not of $\underline{X}$, is a particular distribution of the individuals in $\underline{Y}$ (different percentages of cases belonging to various levels of $\underline{Y}$).

Based on differences of this kind, we estimate the inequality of opportunity as a function of social background with regard to access to effective general education: the percentage of UC members having a satisfactory level compared to the percentage of WC members of the same level, etc. (Tables 18 and 19, page 101).

The influence of the explanatory variable ($\underline{X}$) tends, however, to cause the mean level in $\underline{Y}$ of the members of each of the categories which $\underline{X}$ entails to vary. The between-group variance is a measure of these effects. This variance is the share of variance which is *explained* by the variable $\underline{X}$.

*   *   *

Now $\underline{V} = \underline{V}_{within} + \underline{V}_{between}$.

The validity of this can be verified by observing that for each member of $\underline{P}$, the distance between his position in $\underline{Y}$ and the overall mean of $\underline{Y}$ is equal to the distance between his position in $\underline{Y}$ and the mean of $\underline{Y}$ specific to his category in $\underline{X}$, plus the distance between the mean specific to his category in $\underline{X}$ and the overall mean of $\underline{Y}$. Example: an individual of the MC category whose level in Table 17 is sufficient (3 points).

Within-group difference	+	Between-group difference	=	Total difference
3 - 1.901		1.901-1.896		3-1.896
1.099		0.005		
	1.104		=	1.104

*   *   *

Another example: a member of the WC group whose level is mediocre (1 point).

Within-group difference	+	Between-group difference	=	Total difference
1 - 1.754		1.754 - 1.896		1 - 1.896
-0.754		-0.142		
	-0.896		=	-0.896

*   *   *

The ratio $\underline{V}_{between}/\underline{V}$ indicates the portion of total variance ($\underline{V}$) explained by $\underline{X}(\underline{V}_{between})$. It is this result which the calculation of eta^2 gives:

$$eta^2 = \frac{\underline{V}_{between}}{\underline{V}} = \frac{\text{explained variance}}{\text{total variance}}$$

The other ratio ($\underline{V}_{within}/\underline{V}$) indicates the unexplained portion. This is the portion due to influences independent of $\underline{X}$.

*   *   *

In the real example above (Table 17 onwards), the total variance is 0.83. This corresponds in terms of standard deviation to 0.91, that is, nearly one point.

On the average, therefore, given the combined effect of all causes both between-group and within-group, individuals, rather than having the same level in the subject under consideration (1.896) points), deviate by nearly 1 point. Summarized as a mean, this is the range of the differences(inequality) to be fractioned into two parts: the extent of the differences of level due to differences of category in $\underline{X}$ and the remainder, that is, the range of differences due to all the influences which are independent of $\underline{X}$.

The application by computer of the ad hoc formula - not given here - shows what the ratio $\underline{V}_{between}/\underline{V}$ or eta^2 equals 0.029. Namely, that $\underline{V}_{between}/\underline{V}$ is one thirty-fourth of the total variance $\underline{V}$. More conveniently stated: 2.9%

In our example, this is the crude explanatory impact (share of explained variance) due to social background. The remaining share, 97.1%, is the share

Figure 6. Between group and within group differences in a real situation

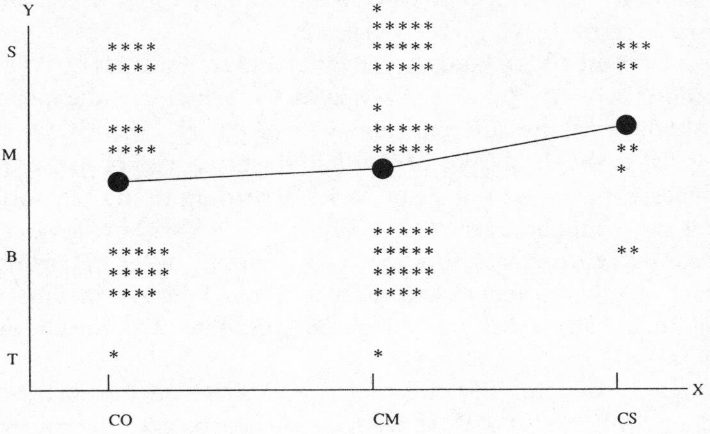

Data drawn from tables 17 to 25

X = explanatory variable (social origin): WC, working class; MC, middle class; UC, upper class.

Y = dependent variable (reading level): VP (very poor, 0 points); P (poor, 1 point); M (mediocre, 2 points); S (satisfactory, 3 points).

* = twenty five individuals

● = average score for the members of three social groups.

$\underline{V}_{within}$. It is the share which differences of social background - as defined in Table 17 - do not explain.

This is the portion due to the range of the differences of level which arise from influences independent of differences in social background; that is, showing in an average number of cases the same degree of influence for all social categories.

Figure 6 summarizes the data contained in Tables 17 and 25. It gives a graphic depiction of the relationship between social background and level of knowledge in our real example. According to Figure 6, it is evident that the explanatory impacts which we have just discussed do reflect reality. Within-group differences do, indeed, exceed by far between-group differences. The former result from the dispersion of cases of identical social class origin, the latter from deviations from the mean per social category.

*　　　*　　　*

The square root of eta^2 gives the coefficient eta, which indicates the extent to which the rank of individuals in $\underline{Y}$ tends to change in relation to their membership in $\underline{X}$. Eta^2 is expressed in terms of variance; its square root is expressed in terms of standard deviations.

The coefficient eta is a kind of correlation index. If there is no dependence (correlation) between $\underline{X}$ and $\underline{Y}$, eta is zero. In such a case, the mean of $\underline{Y}$ is identical within all the different categories of $\underline{X}$.

The smaller the deviations of $\underline{Y}$ within the categories of $\underline{X}$, the closer eta approaches 1, provided the mean varies according to the categories of $\underline{X}$. The limit of 1 would be reached if the differences in $\underline{Y}$ within a given category of $\underline{X}$ disappeared, whereas the mean of $\underline{Y}$ would differ according to the categories of $\underline{X}$. In our real example, the level of all the WC members would be 1.754, that of all the MC members 1.901, and that of all the UC members 2.272.

Eta merely denotes the effect of the variable on the distribution of individuals in $\underline{Y}$, whilst eta^2, as we have seen, separates the causes of this same distribution into two parts: that due to $\underline{X}(V_{between})$ and that due to all the causes which are not dependent on $\underline{X}(V_{within})$.

*   *   *

The two indices (eta and eta^2) can be interpreted in terms of the proportional reduction of the predictive error (PRE) of $\underline{Y}$ values thanks to the knowledge of the values of $\underline{X}$.

Let us suppose that we need to predict the score in reading comprehension (reading exercises from the example in the Annex to Chapters II to V) according to the category of social origin ($\underline{X}$). The most reasonable solution would be to attribute to each member of the population under consideration the average score of his social category. This gives us, according to our real example, 1.754 points for individuals in the WC category, 1.901 for the MC category, and 2.272 for the UC category.

If we had to predict the score of the same individuals without knowing their social background, the safest solution would be to assign to all of them the overall average, 1.896 points.

The error would be greater in the second case than in the first. The reduction of error is proportional to the ratio $\underline{V}_{between}/\underline{V}$.

Indeed, in the first case, the predicted values are nearer the real values, insofar as the dispersion ($\underline{V}_{within}$) is less in each category in relation to its mean than ($\underline{V}$) in relation to the overall mean.

On the basis of the coefficient eta, the reduction of the overall variation in $\underline{Y}$ takes the form of the ratio between group-standard deviation/total standard-deviation in the units of measure of $\underline{Y}$. This ratio indicates the effect of the differences of category in $\underline{X}$ on the average distance (in the sense of the standard deviation) of cases in relation to the overall mean of the $\underline{Y}$ values.

Using eta^2, the proportion of this effect is estimated in terms of variance.

* * *

The advantage of the coefficient eta is that it corresponds to our units of measurement. However, caution must be exercised in interpreting this index. A coefficient eta of 0.800, for example, does not mean that the margin of error is reduced by 80%, nor that, on the scale of explanatory impacts, the differences in $\underline{X}$ explain 80% of the range of the differences in $\underline{Y}$. Nor does a coefficient of 0.800 mean that the dependence in question is four-times stronger that when the eta index is 0.200.

The coefficient eta^2 is clearer. A coefficient eta^2 of 80% would indicate the margin of error is reduced by 80% (or that the impact of the differences in $\underline{X}$ explain the range of the differences in $\underline{Y}$ by a factor of 80%). A coefficient eta^2 of 80% would correspond to a dependence four-times as great as a coefficient of 20%.

Table 15 gives indications illustrating the relationship between the two indices.

These indices only intersect at the extremes: null dependence or perfect dependence.

At degree zero, knowledge of the membership in $\underline{X}$ does not enable us to predict better the rank in $\underline{Y}$. The two entities are totally distinct. At the other extreme, the classification by $\underline{X}$ makes it possible to predict with

---

Table 15. Comparison of percentages and coefficients

ETA^2	$\sqrt{\text{ETA}^2} = \text{ETA}$
0	0
1%	0.1
4%	0.2
25%	0.5
64%	0.8
81%	0.9
100%	1

certainty the position in $\underline{Y}$. The membership in $\underline{X}$ implies the position in $\underline{Y}$. The latter can be deduced without exception from the former. Statistically speaking, the classification by $\underline{X}$ completely determines the rank in $\underline{Y}$, and explains it of and by itself.

Between these two extremes, the implication (or explanation) is only partial, to varying degrees and the two indices give different pictures of this.

A coefficient eta^2 of 25% indicates that one-quarter of the spread of differences in $\underline{Y}$ are explained by the variable $\underline{X}$ (or that knowing $\underline{X}$ reduces by one-quarter the margin of error in predicting $\underline{Y}$). But, the corresponding coefficient eta is halfway between the maximum and the minimum, which could give the - erroneous - impression that we have half of the explanation or that the margin of error is reduced by half.

Square linear correlation (coefficient of determination)

The objective is the same, namely, to estimate the ratio 'explained differences/differences to be explained'. The approach is different.

The two variables must be metric or be made metric.

Figure 7 gives an illustration of the meaning of analysis of explained variance using square linear correlation. We will again use the two variables from our real example, variable $\underline{X}$ (social background) and $\underline{Y}$ (level in reading comprehension).

$\underline{Y}$ ($\underline{Y}$ bar) represents the overall mean of $\underline{Y}$ (the mean level of the total population $\underline{P}$ in reading ability). $\underline{Y}$ ($\underline{Y}$ carat) represent the fitted line (least squares method or straight regression line).

The individuals in each social category ($\underline{X}$) are situated at different levels in $\underline{Y}$, as Table 17 and Figure 6 show. The straight regression line is that in relation to which the (vertical) distance with respect to all individual levels is least. It is thus the line passing the least far (in terms of vertical deviations) from all the points representing individual positions. It is situated at the estimated mean level (of $\underline{Y}$) of the members of this category vertically from each category in $\underline{X}$. It thus translates the between-group differences.

If there were no difference of level in $\underline{Y}$, all the individuals would be found on one line, whatever their origin might be. The level of all of these individuals would be equal to the mean level. They would thus all lie on the line $\underline{Y}$. This is the integral null hypothesis: no difference of level in $\underline{Y}$, meaning the social background ($\underline{X}$) had no effect. The level ($\underline{Y}$) will have gone from being a variable and to being a constant.

Let us suppose, to take another extreme, that the differences in level actually recorded were a linear function (for every increase in $\underline{X}$, an equi-

Figure 7. Portion of explained differences based on linear correlation

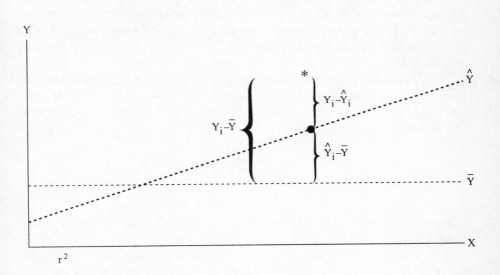

$\overline{Y}$ = overall mean level in $\underline{Y}$ of members of the population P

Y2 = straight regression line of the same means in $\underline{Y}$, but in relation to the classification of individuals in terms of their membership in X.

Y_i-$\overline{Y}$ = total deviation in relation to the overall mean of an individual i.

Y_i1-$\overline{Y}$ = portion of this individual deviation due to the individual's membership in X.

Y_i-Y_i1 = portion of the same individual deviation which is independent of the membership in X.

Y_i-$\overline{Y}$ = (Y_i1-$\overline{Y}$)+(Y_i-Y_i1)

● = estimate of the mean position in $\underline{Y}$ of individuals belonging to the same category as the individual i.

r^2 = Pearson square linear correlation. Ratio of the squares of the between-group deviations (Y1-$\overline{Y}$) to the squares of the means of individual deviations ($\underline{Y}$-$\overline{Y}$) = V$_{between}$/V. That is, the ratio of between-group variance to total variance. Concerns the total population P.

* = Y_i (an individual's position in $\underline{Y}$).

valent increase in $\underline{Y}$) exclusively of $\underline{X}$: all the cases would be on the same line $\underline{Y}$. Only differences in the category $\underline{X}$, that is, the within-group differences, would have an effect.

In reality, for a given category $\underline{X}$, the individual levels in $\underline{Y}$ vary. Within-group differences thus join up with the between-group differences as reflected by the fact that the means per category do not form a straight line. These means are estimated, as we have said, according to a straight line regression.

The Pearson square coefficient of linear correlation indicates the relation between the estimate ($\underline{Y}$) of the between-group differences, and total variance ($\underline{V}$) of the distribution of individuals in $\underline{Y}$ in relation to the general mean $\underline{Y}$. This coefficient is written r^2.

Thus:

$$r^2 = \frac{V_{between}}{\underline{V}} = \frac{\text{explained variance}}{\text{total variance}}$$

In our real example (Table 21) according to the square linear correlation, the share ($V_{between}$) of the differences of social background is 2.6%. The share (V_{within}) due to the influence of factors unrelated to social background is 97.4%. This explanatory impact is nearly identical to that given by eta^2.

* * *

The linear correlation (r) indicates to what extent, overall, under the effect of all the between-group and within-group influences present, the scatter chart representing the distribution of individuals tends to form an ellipse around the straight regression line. Linear correlation is based on standard deviation. Squared (r^2), it is translated into terms of variance.

The correlation r oscillates from 0 to 1 (-1 if the relation is linearly negative: for every increment of increase in $\underline{X}$, an equivalent decrease in $\underline{Y}$).

If the effect of $\underline{X}$ is purely linear, all the cases, as already said, would be on the straight regression line $\underline{Y}$. The ellipse would disappear to be replaced by this line. If the effect of $\underline{X}$ is null, the points tend to be dispersed around the general mean ($\underline{Y}$) no matter what the category in $\underline{X}$. Provided there are cases at all levels of $\underline{Y}$, the scatter chart occupies the entire space.

Between-group influences tend to concentrate the scattering around $\underline{Y}$, while within-group factors tend to make it spread out. The correlation r and the coefficient eta have analogous significance.

As with eta^2, r^2 breaks down the recorded global correlation into two parts, the part due to all $\underline{X}$-related influences ($\underline{V}_{between}$) and all the influences independent of $\underline{X}$ ($\underline{V}_{within}$)

In their substance, the remarks made above concerning the relative significance of the eta and eta^2 with regard to the reduction of the prediction error and the graph of explanatory impacts are valid for correlations (r and r^2).

Multivariate analyses (path and step-wise regression)

The objective remains the same: to dissociate explained differences from unexplained differences. However, rather than a single explanatory variable, two or more are considered. We will examine two methods: path analysis, and stepwise regression.

Path analysis

Path analysis estimates the impact of several explanatory variables ($\underline{X}_1$, $\underline{X}_2$, $\underline{X}_3$, $\underline{X}_4$, etc.) on each other, as well as the effect they have individually and collectively on a dependent variable ($\underline{Y}$). What the global impact of $\underline{X}_1$, $\underline{X}_2$, $\underline{X}_3$, $\underline{X}_4$, etc. on $\underline{Y}$ does not explain is also indicated (unexplained share, that of the independent influence on $\underline{Y}$ of $\underline{X}_1$ as well as $\underline{X}_2$, $\underline{X}_3$, $\underline{X}_4$, etc. Secondarily, the analysis indicates, for example, the share of observed differences in $\underline{X}_4$ which are not explained by $\underline{X}_1$, $\underline{X}_2$ and $\underline{X}_3$.

In a path model, the explanatory variables are dealt with in the order in which they are likely to have begun intervening in reality.

Let us consider a three-explanatory-variable model involving real data. They will again be the reading level of a generation of young men (those in the Annex to Chapters II to V).

The elements of the model are:

$\underline{X}_1$ = *Family - educational background*. Social background (parental educational background aspect; expressed in formal level of education of father.) Three levels, points so as to facilitate calculation of linear correlations: 1 point, no diploma; 2 points, professional diploma; 3 points, high-school diploma or equivalent, including university degrees.

$\underline{X}_2$ = *Family - social class*. Social background (social category aspect; socio-professional category of father): 1 point, working class; 2 points, middle class; 3 points, upper class.

Figure 8: three-variable explanatory model

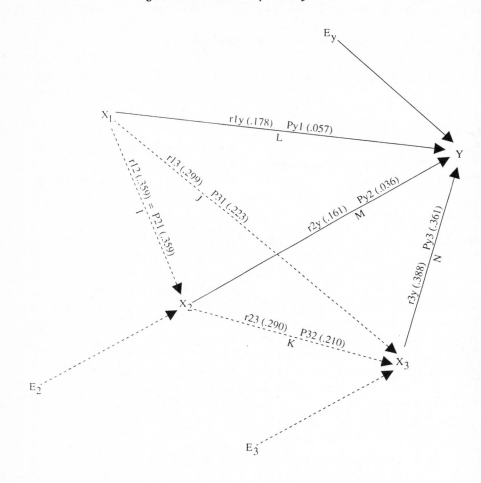

$\underline{X}_1$ (Family educational background). Unaffected by any variable in the model. Acts on $\underline{X}_2$, $\underline{X}_3$ and $\underline{Y}$.

$\underline{X}_2$ (Family social class). Variable influenced by $\underline{X}_1$. Acts on $\underline{X}_3$ and $\underline{Y}$.

$\underline{X}_3$ (Diplomas). Variable influenced by $\underline{X}_1$ and $\underline{X}_2$. Acts on $\underline{Y}$.

$\underline{E}_2$ Unidentified influences. Act on $\underline{X}_2$, independently of $\underline{X}_1$.

$\underline{E}_3$ Unidentified influences. Act on $\underline{X}_3$, independently of $\underline{X}_1$ and $\underline{X}_2$.

$\underline{E}_y$ Unidentified influences. Act on $\underline{Y}$, independently of $\underline{X}_1$, $\underline{X}_2$ and $\underline{X}_3$

$\underline{Y}$ Knowledge. Level (in reading, according to the annexe to chapters II to IV).

$\underline{X}_3$ = *Qualifications*. Type of training of those interviewed. Their formal level of education. Three levels. The same as for the father.

$\underline{Y}$ = *Level*. One aspect of real knowledge. Reading ability. Scores from a series of questions making up a reading comprehension exercise. Same young adults. Very poor, 0; poor, 1; mediocre, 2; satisfactory, 3.

Graphically the model has the form shown in Figure 8. On each arrow, the correlation (r) is on the left, the Path coefficient ($\underline{P}$) is to the right (see Table 28). For example, r_{13} = the correlation of $\underline{X}_1$ with $\underline{X}_3$; $\underline{P}_{31}$ = the path coefficient of $\underline{X}_1$ with $\underline{X}_3$.

In Figure 8, the influences are represented by arrows. The influences corresponding to phases up until the end of school attendance are indicated by arrows with broken lines. Arrows with solid lines indicate the impact on each level of knowledge.

*   *   *

The calculations are done in stages. Each relates to a given problem. At each step the calculations produce ratios, corresponding to different points of view.

$$\frac{\text{Explained variance}}{\text{total variance}} = \frac{V_{\text{between}}}{V}$$

Figure 9. Stages in path analysis

Step 1.	Step 2.	Step 3
Schooling and social status. Fathers	Inequality of educational opportunity. Young men.	Social background (two aspects), schooling and knowledge (one aspect). Young men.

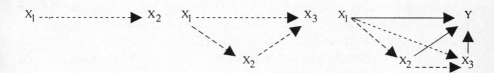

Here are a few indications concerning these calculations.

First step. Since there is no intermediate variable between X_1 and X_2, we need simply to record (arrow I) the correlation between the first variable coming into play with the first (X_1), followed by the second (X_2). The correlation here is 0.359.

This corresponds to a crude explanatory impact (0.359^2) of 12.9%. In this proportion, the formal level of education explains, on average, the differences (variances) of social category, as concerns the fathers. These differences are, therefore, 87.1% - that is, around seven-times - more dependent on a complete set of factors (E_2) which are independent of X_1.

The crude explanatory impact of X_1 comprises all the effects which this variable exerts directly and indirectly on X_2. Directly: in the strictest sense of the term, effects of diplomas on hiring and career advancement, for example. Indirectly: the higher the level of the diploma, the greater the chances that the social background, skills, etc., will also be high and that in turn, these attributes have a more favourable influence on career.

The correlation between X_1 and X_2 is used in the following calculation to dissociate the influences of these two variables on X_3 and Y.

Second step. From here, the influences of certain variables are dissociated.

The second step consists in estimating the impact which the model's two aspects (X_1 and X_2) related to social background have on the formal level of education (X_3).

Let us begin with the direct impacts and net impacts.

Direct impact of X_1 on X_3 (that accounted for by X_1 - more precisely, by all the influences varying more or less systematically in terms of rank in X_1, controlling for X_2). Arrow j. The indirect effect of X_1 on X_3 via X_2 is left aside.

Direct impact of X_2 on X_3 (same, controlling for X_1). Arrow k.

This second step involves the solving of a system of equations in order to determine the unknowns P_{31} and P_{32}. This involves partial correlations (correlations between two variables, once their relation with one or more than one other variables has been controlled). Controlling for the effects of a variable involves standardizing them, on the assumption that individuals are similar with regard to these variables.

The coefficients thus obtained are termed *beta coefficients* or, in the context of path analysis, *path coefficients*.

In the present case, one variable (X_2) is controlled to obtain P_{31} and a another one (X_1) to obtain P_{32}.

The equations give:

$\underline{P}_{31} = 0.223$; $\underline{P}_{32} = 0.210$.

The direct explanatory impact of $\underline{X}_1$ (part of variance - of $\underline{X}_3$ - which is explained by $\underline{X}_1$) is (0.223^2) 5.0%. That of $\underline{X}_2$ (part of variance - of $\underline{X}_3$ - which is explained by $\underline{X}_2$) is (0.210^2) of 4.4%. The direct impacts being distinct, they can be added.

Another calculation - more common - is that of the impacts which here we will call 'net'. This calculation involves splitting up the square coefficient of multiple correlation $(R^2_{3.21})$ which translates the share of variance of $\underline{X}_3$ which is explained by the total combined effect of the variables $\underline{X}_1$ and $\underline{X}_2$, both direct and indirect.

Calculating a coefficient of multiple correlation involves not only the direct effect of the explanatory variables present, but also their interdependence (intercorrelations). Thus, here, they account for the fact that the higher the level of the individuals in $\underline{X}_1$, the greater are the chances of the level also being high under $\underline{X}_2$ and that, consequently, the effects of the latter variable play an indirect role in the ratio $\underline{X}_1\underline{X}_3$. And, furthermore, that the ratio $\underline{X}_2\underline{X}_3$ includes the indirect effects of $\underline{X}_1$, for the higher the ranking under $\underline{X}_2$, the higher it will also tend to be under $\underline{X}_1$.

In a path analysis, the net explanatory impact of a variable on another is estimated by calculating the product of the correlation and the path coefficient linking them. The path coefficient represents the direct effect of the first variable on the second (for example, $\underline{P}_{31}$ = the partial correlation, hence direct, of $\underline{X}_1$ and $\underline{X}_3$, controlling for $\underline{X}_2$. The correlation represents the total - direct and indirect - effect of the first variable on the second (here, r_{13} = the correlation between $\underline{X}_1$ and $\underline{X}_3$). The product of these two coefficients gives the net explanatory impact of $\underline{X}_1$ on $\underline{X}_3$ (proportion of variance of $\underline{X}_3$ explained by $\underline{X}_1$). The same applies to $\underline{X}_2$. This procedure is a means of attributing to each of the explanatory variables present its individual share of the combined impact.

Thus, the influence of $\underline{X}_1$ and $\underline{X}_2$ on $\underline{X}_3$: the net explanatory impact of $\underline{X}_1$ on $\underline{X}_3$ (0.299 x 0.223) + the net explanatory impact of $\underline{X}_2$ on $\underline{X}_3$ (0.290 x 0.210) = $R^2_{3.12}$ (square multiple correlation of $\underline{X}_1$ and of $\underline{X}_2$ with $\underline{X}_3$). In percentages, 6.7% + 6.1% = 12.8%.

Together, via their net impacts, the two aspects of social background under consideration explain 12.8% of the differences (variances) in the kind of schooling received ($\underline{X}_3$). There remains an impact of 87.2% for all the factors which are independent of $\underline{X}_1$ and $\underline{X}_2$.

The net explanatory impacts can be added together because they are distinct.

This is not the case with crude explanatory impacts. The crude explanatory impact $\underline{X}_1$ on $\underline{X}_3$ ($r^2_{13} = 0.299^2 = 8.9\%$) includes, among other indirect effects, all those which are channelled via $\underline{X}_2$. These effects are real and it is thus normal that they be included in the crude explanatory impact of $\underline{X}_1$ on $\underline{X}_3$. But some of them also have a part in the crude impact of $\underline{X}_2$ on $\underline{X}_3$ (0.290 = 8.4%). Adding these two crude explanatory impacts together would give a misleading figure. Fractioning is necessary if we wish to analyse the impact (R^2) which two variables or more have on another. The calculation of the net impacts is for this purpose. It assigns to each explanatory variable, in addition to its direct effects, its proportion of indirect effects, without overlapping.

Third step. The same principles apply. Estimation of the direct, partial effects of $\underline{X}_1$, $\underline{X}_2$, and $\underline{X}_3$ on $\underline{Y}$. With respect to the direct effects, the equations give the following:

$\underline{P}_{Y1} = 0.057 \; 0.057^2 = 0.3\%$ (Arrow L);

$\underline{P}_{Y2} = 0.036 \; 0.036^2 = 0.1\%$ (Arrow M);

$\underline{P}_{Y3} = 0.0361 \; 0.0361^2 = 13.0\%$ (Arrow N).

The total = 13.4%.

In terms of net effects and the (square) coefficient of multiple correlation, the equations give:

of $\underline{X}_1$ on $\underline{Y}$: $0.178 \times 0.057 = 1.0\%$ (Arrow L);

of $\underline{X}_2$ on $\underline{Y}$: $0.161 \times 0.036 = 0.6\%$ (Arrow M);

of $\underline{X}_3$ on $\underline{Y}$: $0.388 \times 361 = 14.0\%$ (Arrow N).

Total: $R^2_{Y.123} = 15.6\%$.

The sum of the direct explanatory impacts make up the major share of the total impact ($R^2_{Y.123}$) in this case. Little is left for the indirect explanatory impacts (15.6 - 13.4 = 2.2%).

*   *   *

In the second step, the step which corresponds to the problem of educational inequality, the social background ($\underline{X}_1$ and $\underline{X}_2$) did indeed exert an influence (Arrows J and K) on the course of events and, hence, ultimately on the formal level of education ($\underline{X}_3$).

But, in the third step, the effect of these variables on knowledge ($\underline{Y}$) in our example shrinks to virtually nothing. Only the differences of formal level more or less tend to cause the latter to vary, but in rather limited proportions.

Figure 10. Separation of explanatory impacts using the path method

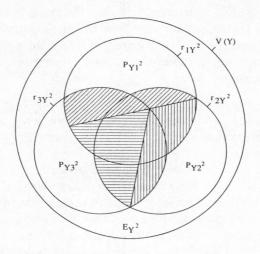

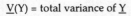

$\underline{V}(Y)$ = total variance of $\underline{Y}$

$\underline{r}_1Y^2$ = crude explanatory impact of $\underline{X}_1$ on $\underline{Y}$.

$\underline{r}_2Y^2$ = crude explanatory impact of $\underline{X}_2$ on $\underline{Y}$.

$\underline{r}_3Y^2$ = crude explanatory impact of $\underline{X}_3$ on $\underline{Y}$.

$\underline{P}_{Y1}^2$ = direct explanatory impact of $\underline{X}_1$ on $\underline{Y}$.

$\underline{P}_{Y2}^2$ = direct explanatory impact of $\underline{X}_2$ on $\underline{Y}$.

$\underline{P}_{Y3}^2$ = direct explanatory impact of $\underline{X}_3$ on $\underline{Y}$.

Shaded parts   = indirect effects of $\underline{X}_1$, $\underline{X}_2$ and $\underline{X}_3$ on $\underline{Y}$. Those represented by circle $\underline{r}_1Y^2$ are part of the crude explanatory impact of $\underline{X}_1$. Those represented by circle $\underline{r}_2Y^2$ are part of the crude explanatory impact of $\underline{X}_2$. Those represented by circle $\underline{r}_3Y^2$ are part of the crude explanatory impact of of $\underline{X}_3$.

     ▨   = fraction of the shaded portion attributed by the analysis to the net explanatory impact of $\underline{X}_1$.

     ▥   = fraction of the shaded portion attributed by the analysis to the net explanatory impact of $\underline{X}_2$.

     ▤   = fraction of the shaded portion attributed by the analysis to the net explanatory impact of $\underline{X}_3$.

The total impact corresponding to the multiple correlation ($R^2_{Y.123}$) of $\underline{X}_1$, $\underline{X}_2$, and $\underline{X}_3$ with $\underline{Y}$ explains 15.6% of the differences (variance of $\underline{Y}$). This leaves 84.4% for the independent factors (E_2) of the model. The various, undetermined causes designated by E_y are therefore, in the present case, five to six times less influential than those tied to these three variables.

Figure 10 shows the kind of distribution which the path method gives, but we did not attempt to make the areas in it proportional to the numerical data of the preceding pages.

Stepwise regression

Stepwise regression is another method of fractioning the combined effects (multiple correlation) of several explanatory variables ($\underline{X}_1$, $\underline{X}_2$, $\underline{X}_3$ in our example) on the dependent variable ($\underline{Y}$).

At each step, the analysis records the explanatory impact of a variable by controlling those which have already been considered. For example, we might begin with the last variable in the process, go on to the second last, and so on. This is what will be done here, to retain the structure of the model on the preceding pages. Or, as another possibility, we might begin with the variable whose effect is greatest, followed in descending order of magnitude of effect by the remaining variables. This enables us to eliminate the variables which have virtually no effect and to focus our attention on the others when attempting to refine the explanation.

We will begin, then, with the effect of $\underline{X}_3$ (diplomas), followed by $\underline{X}_2$ (family/social category) and, lastly, $\underline{X}_1$ (family/educational background). The effect of the first variable, as analysed by stepwise regression, is simply estimated according to its linear correlation with the dependent variable. Here, the correlation $\underline{X}_3$ (diplomas) with $\underline{Y}$ (level in basic mathematics) is 0.388. That gives an initial explanatory impact (0.388^2) of 15.1%.

Once this is done, the analysis records the multiple correlation ($R_{Y2.3}$) obtained by introducing $\underline{X}_2$ (family/social category). The difference indicates the effect due to $\underline{X}_2$: the effect of $\underline{X}_2$ in the same category under $\underline{X}_3$.

It remains to record the multiple correlation ($R_{Y1.23}$) obtained by introducing $\underline{X}_1$ (family/educational background): the effect of $\underline{X}_1$ in the same category under $\underline{X}_2$ and $\underline{X}_3$.

This gives the results shown in Table 16.

Accordingly, if we combine all the influences of differences in social background ($\underline{X}_1$ and $\underline{X}_2$) and of the kind of training ($\underline{X}_3$), they explain 15.6% of the differences of level ($\underline{Y}$) in the reading exercise presented in the tables in the Annex to Chapters II to V.

Table 16. Stepwise regression.

	R (multiple correlation with Y)	R^2 ($\underline{Y}_{between}/\underline{Y}$)	Increment R^2 added at each stage (explanatory impact of the added variable)	Unexplained portion ($\underline{Y}_{within}/\underline{Y}$)	Total (%)
$\underline{X}_3$ (diplomas)	0.388	15.1%	15.1%	84.9%	100
Plus $\underline{X}_2$ (family social class)	0.391	15.3%	0.2	84.7%	100
Plus $\underline{X}_1$ (family educational background)	0.395	15.6%	0.3%	84.4%	100

This percentage is identical to that which was obtained above using the path method. The picture of the structure of influences is nonetheless quite similar in terms of magnitudes.

Notes

1. We wish to express our gratitude to Professor Gilbert Ritschard (Department of Econometrics, University of Geneva) for his invaluable comments on this section.

CHAPTER FIVE

Inequality of opportunity and explanatory impacts

The chances of achieving a good level in a subject or the risk of only achieving a poor level can vary considerably between some of the groups defined by social class, even when the latter only partially explains the general ranking of individuals according to their levels in the subject. The same is true of the effect of kind of current schooling and of the formal level of education (adults, kind of schooling completed). It is very easy to understand why.

Inequality of opportunity based on social background or analogous differences related to kind of schooling can be evaluated most directly by comparing subsets, usually small subsets, for attention is thus focused on the special cases.

Explanatory impacts, in contrast, are calculated on the scale of the entire sample. Though less eloquent than would be the comparison of subsets, they also give an idea of the inequality of opportunity.

We will limit our discussion to the example used above: young men (Switzerland, 1987), level in reading comprehension (data in the tables following the present chapter).

Let us begin with the *effect of differences of social background*, namely, working class, middle class and upper class.

The most common presentation of the data is that given in Table 18. The table deals with social mobility, in particular: the proportion of the members of each social category according to the category they belong to as adults. This gives us an indication of their outlook in terms of social advancement:

to what extent does the social category attained differ according to the social category of departure?

We are concerned here with the distribution of knowledge, not that of occupations. The question we ask is: to what extent does the level of knowledge differ depending on social background?

Table 18 highlights some of these differences. In particular it shows that, for the subject chosen in the example, the proportion of young men of upper-class origin demonstrating a satisfactory level in the subject (column I/D) is nearly twice that of the sons of working-class parents with the same level in the subject (column III/D).

Table 19 brings these differences out more clearly.

In the following table, Table 20, the problem is approached from the point of view of enrolment. This approach provides many indications concerning the inequality of educational opportunity: for example, the percentage of children of blue-collar workers, white-collar workers, etc., attending university in comparison with the total enrolment. The question then is: to what extent do social backgrounds differ within groups defined according to the educational institution attended (or the level of scholastic achievement, diplomas)?.

The percentages obtained are a function of both the size of a particular social class group and the effects of the selection process, which vary according to social class. The conclusions drawn on this basis must take these two parameters into consideration. It may happen, for example, that because economic and social development can result in the - relative or absolute - shrinking of a social category, the proportion of young people of this background would drop in relation to the total number of students at university, whereas the chances of attending university increase for young people of this background.

Table 20 shows that the three social categories of our classification are all represented at every level of knowledge, most often in statistically rather normal proportions, that is, consistent with their proportion in the population. This observation already suggests that ultimately, the effect of social background is perhaps not significant on an overall scale.

This is confirmed by Table 21. If the relationship background/level of knowledge were absolute, each social category would have a level at which all its members and they alone would be grouped. The two indices of Table 21 (eta and linear correlation) would be 1. If, on the contrary, the effect of background on level was nil (same distribution per level for each background), the two indices would be zero. In fact, they are far closer to this lower limit than to the upper limit.

In terms of the crude explanatory impact (proportion of explained variance), the relationship background/level is very small: 2.6 to 2.9%. Using a reading comprehension exercise as an example, the differences in level depend almost entirely on factors other than social background, as was observed and explained in Chapter IV. Tables 22 to 24 show that this is totally consistent with real-life situations.

Let us recall that explanatory impacts indicate the extent to which the real distributional structure deviates from what would be expected if the explanatory variable or variables had no effect on the dependent variable. The absence of effect is what the so-called 'null hypothesis' postulates.

Table 22 gives the theoretical distribution which would correspond to the null hypothesis. Here, the result would be total equality of opportunity according to social background.

Table 23 is the result of comparison of theoretical and real distributions (of Table 17). The classification of only 116 cases would need to be changed for the latter (real) distribution to be identical with the former (equality of opportunity). The classifications of the 2,064 others could remain the same. Their distribution according to level already corresponds to what would result if differences of social background had no effect. Table 24 also illustrates, in another fashion, the fact that, overall, the real distribution and the distribution according to the null hypothesis are rather similar.

If reality corresponded to the null hypothesis, the mean level of the members of each social background category would be identical. In fact, this mean differs little, especially where the categories comprising the vast majority of the sample population are concerned (Table 25).

The distances between averages are, to borrow the wording of Chapter III, the effect of between-group differences of background. In the example used - but the phenomenon is general - the smallness of the explanatory impacts obtained is due to the fact that differences of level of knowledge are nearly always within-group differences (of background). The computation of the correlations and crude explanatory impacts brings this out more clearly. Multivariate analysis does as well.

Inequality of opportunity, too, is no less real. It is customarily evaluated by comparing two kinds of case: the sub-group made up of the most favoured in terms of social background who attained the particular goal chosen for the analysis (depending on the field: secondary school diploma, a top management post, for example, or, as in the present case, a satisfactory level of knowledge in a given subject), and the sub-group of those least favoured in terms of social background who achieved the same goal. These two sub-groups are generally rather small. The first one represents a fraction of the most highly privileged minority. The second is comprised of only relatively exceptional cases. In our example (Table 17), the first group (column I/D) represents 6.1% of the population and the second (III/D), 9.4%. The observations which can be made regarding them are entirely valid and are indicative of the degree of inequality of opportunity. The first sub-group represents slightly more than half of the contingent of young men of upper-class origin and the second, only slightly more than one-quarter of the sons of blue-collar workers. Thus, it is undeniable that being raised in an upper-class environment doubles the chances of achieving the given goal over those of an individual of working-class origin.

When the situation is examined from this point of view, the remaining distributions are of little interest. At times, however, the case of the lowest ranked is considered. In our example (Table 19), the persons in group I (upper class) are one-half as likely to be situated at a 'very poor' level as the individuals in group III (working class). Yet, the two subsets in this comparison (I/A and III/A) are especially small (0.2% and 1.1% of those tested, Table 17).

The above comparisons only concern four cells (I/D, I/A, III/D, and III/A) of the tables given. Category II, which constitutes the majority, namely, the middle class, is completely left out. These categories also fail to take into account two-thirds of working-class children, namely those whose level is neither very high nor very low, nor satisfactory, but is the most frequently encountered (level B or C). They also leave out those of group I (upper class) who are at levels B and C (nearly half of the young people in this social category).

In contrast, when the explanatory impacts are calculated, the entire set is taken into consideration. What they tell us is just as undeniable as the inequality of opportunity between opposite sub-groups. The overall distribution of individuals is not affected to a great extent by the inequality of opportunity between these sub-groups. The general distribution differs little from what total equality of opportunity or the absence of dependence between differences of background and differences of level would give. In other words, the situation in which these differences - great or small, which translate into very poor, mediocre, or acceptable mean levels - would be entirely of a within-group nature, as defined in Chapter III. Total absence of differences of level (everyone at the same, preferably good, level) is the limit of the equality of opportunity. *The effect of the formal level of education* is markedly greater than that of social background (Tables 26 and 27).

As is to be expected, the majority of high-school graduates obtained satisfactory scores according to their performance on the very simple reading exercises of our survey. In contrast, very few members of the minority of those with no diploma do as well. The probability of achieving this level is six times greater for high-school graduates than for individuals without diplomas. But, again, the comparison only concerns two fractions of the total sample population: the first, the small group made up of secondary school graduates having a satisfactory level (17.2% of those surveyed); the second, the tiny group of those with no diploma having the same level (0.5%).

Individuals in possession of vocational school diplomas make up three-quarters of those surveyed. This is the typical case. The general distribution of cases by level (the 'Total' row in Table 26) is naturally rather close to that of this very large group.

Ultimately, at the total sample level, the relationship between formal level of education and real level of knowledge is, in the present case, barely average (eta, 0.401; linear correlation, 0.388, Table 28), giving a crude explanatory impact of between 15.1 and 16.1%. With regard to the relationship between formal level of education and reading comprehension level, if we compare the tables (not reproduced here) which give, in absolute numbers, the theoretical distribution of cases according to the null hypothesis and their real distribution, we find that these two distributions differ relatively little. If only 16.3% of those surveyed were reclassified, the real distribution would be identical with the null hypothesis.

Again, we observe that there is no contradiction: the disparity between the high-school graduate and the individual with no diploma in terms of attainment of a satisfactory level is one aspect of reality; the moderate intercorrelation between the formal level of education and the real level observed for the total population level is another.

Selected data concerning young men (Switzerland, 1984)

As we pointed out at the beginning of Chapter II, this Annex contains the data to which Chapters III to V and passages of Chapter II refer. It comprises tables which can be divided into four groups, namely:

I. *Social background and level in a core curriculum subject - reading* (Tables 17 to 25);

II. *Formal level of education and level in the same subject - reading* (Tables 26 and 27);

III. *Social background (formal level of education of the father, social class), formal level of education and level in the same subject (reading). Correlations and path coefficients* (Table 28).

IV. *Variations of explanatory impacts and correlations according to subject and the degree of refinement of the classification* (Tables 29 to 31).

Table 17. Real level in a general education subject (reading) according to social background category. Young men. Switzerland (1984). Distribution in absolute numbers[1]

Background[2]	Level[3]				Total (%)
	A = very poor (0 points)	B= poor (1 point)	C= mediocre (2 points)	D= satisfactory (3 points)	
I. Upper class	5	52	74	134	265
II. Middle class	27	468	275	406	1176
III. Working class	24	338	173	204	739
Total	56	858	522	744	2180

1. Real distribution, according to a 1984 survey (Girod et al., 1987). The sample population consisted of all (34,907) young men inducted (first part of military service) in 1984 (present the day on which their unit was given the questionnaire). Part I of the questionnaire was completed by all recruits. It asked for the age of the recruit (88% of those tested were between 20 and 21 years old; the others were approximately the same age), the geographical origin, educational background, vocational training, mother's and father's formal level of education, father's socio-professional category. It also included a non-verbal logical reasoning test.

The following part of the questionnaire consisted of eight variants (one of which was subdivided into two sub-categories), each corresponding to a probabilistic sub-sample of the total sample. This made it possible to cover the subjects better and to increase the number of problems and questions. Subjects: reading comprehension (mother tongue); arithmetic and elementary mathematics; basic spelling and grammar; history and geography; national languages (other than the mother tongue); English; art and literature; test of practical and technical reasoning; miscellaneous (scientific knowledge, nature, a few questions concerning definitions of economic and technical terms, as well as on political institutions).

Tables 17-28 refer to only one example, namely, the results of a reading comprehension exercise in the candidate's own language (German, French, Italian, as applicable). Three texts, the difficulty of which did not exceed that of editorials destined for the public at large, were used. These were followed by eleven questions on their content and the meaning of certain expressions or certain passages. In all, 4,231 recruits made up the sample of persons filling out the version of the questionnaire containing this exercise. The analyses presented in Tables 17-28 apply only to those tested who could be classified according to their father's formal level of education and socio-professional category, as well as their own formal level of education. A total of 2,180 cases met this requirement. All Swiss males are subject to military service. With respect to social class and educational background, those who are declared unfit for induction do not differ from the others. Controls have shown that the responses by those tested are extremely reliable.

2. As per father's occupation. Upper class: directors, liberal and related professions, heads of major enterprises. Middle class: small businessmen, farmers, office, white-collar

employees, middle management, primary school-teachers, secondary school-teachers, social workers, technicians, and similar cases. Working class: from labourers to foreman.
3. Failed all eleven exercises - 0 points; correct answers on 1 to 4 exercises - 1 point; on 5 to 6 exercises - 2 points; on 7 to 11 exercises, that is, 2/3 of the exercises - 3 points.

Table 18. Real level in a general education subject (reading) according to social background category. Young males. Switzerland (1984). In %.[1]

Background	Level				Total (%)
	A = very poor	B = poor	C = mediocre	D = satisfactory	
I. Upper class	1.9	19.6	27.9	50.6	100%
II. Middle class	2.3	39.8	23.4	34.5	100%
III. Working class	3.2	45.7	23.4	27.6	100%
Total	2.6	39.4	23.9	34.1	100%

1. As per Table 17. Reads as follows: 50.6% of those tested of upper class origin had satisfactory scores, 27.9% mediocre scores, etc.

Table 19. Real level in a general education subject (reading) according to social background category. Young men. Switzerland (1984). Inequality of opportunity.[1]

Background	Level			
	A = very poor	B = poor	C = mediocre	D = satisfactory
I. Upper class	-1.68	-2.33	+1.19	+1.83
II. Middle class	-1.39	-1.15	-	+1.25
III. Working class	1	1	1	1

1. As per Table 17. Reads as follows: young men of upper class origin are about twice as likely to fall into the satisfactory category as the sons of blue-collar workers (50.6/27.6 = 1.83), and they are one-half as likely to fall into the very poor category (3.2/1.91=1.68), etc.

*Table 20. Social background category according to the real level in a general education
subject (reading). Young men. Switzerland (1984). In %.*[1]

Background	Level				Total (%)
	A = very poor	B = poor	C = mediocre	D = satisfactory	
I. Upper class	8.9	6.1	14.2	18.0	12.2
II. Middle class	48.2	54.5	52.7	54.6	53.9
III. Working class	42.9	39.4	33.1	27.4	33.9
Total	100	100	100	100	100

1. As per Table 17. Reads as follows: 42.9% of those tested whose level was very poor are
the sons of blue-collar workers, 48.2% are from the middle class and 8.9% from the upper
class, etc.

*Table 21. Social background category and real level in a general education subject (reading).
Young men. Switzerland (1984). Level of dependence and crude explanatory impact.*[1]

	According to eta	According to linear correlation
Measure of dependence of reading levels on social background category	eta = 0.17	r = 0.161
Crude explanatory impact (portion of explained variance) of the social background category on differences of level in reading	$eta^2 = 2.9\%$	$r^2 = 2.6\%$

1. As per Table 17. Regarding the nature of these coefficients, see Chapter IV.

Table 22. Social background category and real level in a general education subject (reading). Young men. Switzerland (1984). Theoretical distribution according to the null hypothesis (complete independence on the two variables = complete equality of opportunity).[1]

Background	Level				Total (%)
	A = very poor	B = poor	C = mediocre	D = satisfactory	
I. Upper class	7	104	63	91	265
II. Middle class	30	463	282	401	1176
III. Working class	19	291	177	252	739
Total	56	858	522	744	2180

1. Same overall distribution based on actual data (table 17) according to social class ('Total' column) and level ('Total' row). But in the table, cases are distributed on the assumption of complete equality of opportunity: as a %, same distribution by level no matter what the social background (and, hence, overall) and same distribution by social background, irrespective of level (and, hence, as overall).

Table 23. Social background category and real level in a general education subject (reading). Young men. Switzerland (1984). Cell-by-cell comparison. Deviations between the real distinction and the theoretical distribution based on the null hypothesis (complete independence of the two variables = complete equality of opportunity).[1]

Background	Level			
	A = very poor	B = poor	C = mediocre	D = satisfactory
I. Upper class	-2	-52	+11	+43
II. Middle class	-3	+5	-7	+5
III. Working class	+5	+47	-4	-48

1. As per Tables 17 and 22. On the basis of actual data (table 17), five persons tested are of upper class origin and have scores at the 'very poor' level. In a situation of complete equality of opportunity there should have been seven with such scores. Two cases are thus 'lacking', etc. Since any individual 'in excess' in one entry item will automatically be 'missing' in another, the total of all negative numbers ('missing' individuals) is equal to the total of all positive numbers (individuals 'in excess'), both with respect to row total and column total (and overall). Hence, one must not add the positive and negative numbers to determine the number of cases to be reclassified in order to arrive at a situation of equality of opportunity. It is sufficient to find the sum of one or the other. In the present case, 116 individuals need to change category (5.3% of the total number of cases, which was 2,180).

Table 24. Real level in a general education subject (reading) according to social background category. Young men. Switzerland (1984). Cell-by-cell differences between the real distribution and the theoretical distribution based on the null hypothesis (complete independence of the two variables = complete equality of opportunity).[1]

Background	Level			
	A = very poor	B = poor	C = mediocre	D = satisfactory
I. Upper class	-1.4	-2.0	+1.17	+1.47
II. Middle class	-1.11	+1.01	-1.03	+1.01
III. Working class	-1.26	+1.16	-1.02	-1.24

1. As per Tables 17-22. Reads as follows: if there were equality of opportunity, the group I/D (upper class, satisfactory level) would contain 91 individuals (table 22) rather than 134 (table 17). Group A is 1.5 times better represented at this level (134/91 = 1.47) than if social background had no effect.

Table 25. Real level in a general education subject (reading). On the scale of a generation and according to social background category. Young men. Switzerland (1984).

	Mean level (in points)[1]
I. Upper class	2.272
II. Middle class	1.901
III. Working class	1.754
Total	1.896

1. As per Table 17. For example, upper class:

$$\frac{(5 \times 0 \text{ points}) + (52 \times 1) + (74 \times 2) + (134 \times 3)}{265} = 2.272$$

Table 26. Formal level of education and real level in a general education subject (reading). Young men. Switzerland (1984). Distribution in absolute numbers[1]

Formal level of education	Level				Total
	A = very poor	B = poor	C = mediocre	D = satisfactory	
Secondary school qualification and analogous cases including university	8	71	122	374	575
Vocational qualifications	44	732	377	360	1513
No qualification	4	55	23	10	92
Total	56	858	522	744	2180

1. Same source as Table 17.

Table 27. Real level in a general education subject (reading). Young men. Switzerland (1984). As a percentage[1]

Formal level of education	Level				Total
	A = very poor	B = poor	C = mediocre	D = satisfactory	
Secondary school qualification and analogous cases including university	1.4	12.3	21.2	65.0	100
Vocational qualifications	2.9	48.4	24.9	23.8	100
No qualification	4.3	59.8	25.0	10.9	100
Total	2.6	39.4	23.9	34.1	100

1. As per Table 26. To be read in the same way as Table 18.

Table 28. Social background (two criteria), formal level of education and level in a general education subject (reading). Young men. Switzerland (1984). Correlations and path coefficients[1]

	X_1 Father's formal level of education	X_2 Family's social class (according to father's occupation)	X_3 Formal level of education (of those tested)	Y Level in reading (of those tested)
X_1 Father's formal level of education		0.359^2	0.299 (0.233)	0.178 (0.057)
X_2 Family's social class (according to father's occupation)			0.290 (0.210)	0.161 (0.36)
X_3 Formal level of education (of those tested				0.388 (0.361)
Y Level in reading (of those tested)				

1. Same source, same cases (2,180), same categories as in the preceding tables. Father's formal level of education, same categories as for those tested. Linear correlations (Pearson) with, in parentheses, path coefficients (see Chapter III).
2. No path coefficient here, as the father's formal level of education is the first variable to intervene in the model and the family's social class is the second.

Table 29. Explanatory impact of social background and formal level of education on real levels in various fields, according to multivariate analyses, with % of those tested achieving satisfactory scores in these areas. Young men. Switzerland (1984)[1]

Portion of differences (variance) explained by ...[2]

	Social background[3]	Formal level of education[4]	Total (%)	Overall level (% of men with satisfactory scores[5]
Basic spelling and grammar	0.3	4.7	5.0	81.4
Basic scientific knowledge, nature	0.6	4.6	5.2	64.4
History, geography	0.8	8.7	9.5	25.5
Reading comprehension (mother tongue)	0.8	9.0	9.8	50.7
Arithmetic and elementary mathematics	1.0	13.4	14.4	38.5
Second national language (German or French)	4.6	16.7	21.3	58.6
English	4.5	18.6	23.1	53.1
Art and literature	2.7	25.0	27.7	9.0
Mean[6]	1.9	12.6	14.5	47.7

1. *Source*: survey described in the notes to Table 17. All persons of 20-21 years of age questioned in each sample. Eight fields, in order of increasing total explanatory impact of social background and of formal level of education. Several series of exercises per subject (except for basic spelling and grammar and 'art and literature'), none of which was similar to those of the preceding tables.
2. Net impacts according to multivariate analyses of the type explained in Chapter IV.
3. Cumulative net impacts of 'family-educational background' and of 'family-social class'. Family-educational background (father's formal level of education): 1. no qualifications; 2. vocational school qualification; 3. secondary school qualification and analogous cases (including university). Family-social class: (based on father's occupation): 1. upper class; 2. middle class; 3. working class.
4. Of the person tested. Same categories as for the father.
5. Successfully completed around two-thirds (or more) of the exercises related to the field under consideration.
6. For the eight fields considered here.

Table 30. Dependence (coefficient eta) of the level in various general education subjects in relation to the social background category and the formal level of education, depending on the degree of detail of the classification. Young males. Switzerland (1984)[1]

	Subject								Mean degree of independence
	Reading comprehension (mother tongue)	Arithmetic mathematics	Basic spelling and grammar	History, geography	National languages	English	Art and literature	Misc.	
Social background category[2]									
Two categories	0.093/0.124	0.089/0.113	0.039/0.097	0.93/0.114	0.155/0.193	0.180/0.184	0.187/0.196	0.081/0.101	0.115/0.14
Three	0.097/0.104	0.113/0.117	*/0.062	0.091/0.105	0.186/0.215	0.2/0.225	0.203/0.206	0.091/0.108	0.14/0.148
Eight	0.158/0.198	0.175/0.202	*/0.194	0.149/0.175	0.21/0.309	0.293/0.386	0.252/0.341	0.14/0.141	0.197/0.243
Twenty-two	0.178/0.221	0.202/0.238	*/0.217	0.168/0.205	0.255/0.329	0.292/0.38	0.26/0.349	0.167/0.179	0.217/0.264
Formal level of education[3]									
Two levels	0.211/0.253	0.231/0.267	0.057/0.203	0.21/0.24	0.311/0.401	0.348/0.372	0.34/0.417	0.101/0.417	0.226/0.288
Three	0.266/0.31	0.342/0.385	0.088/0.248	0.278/0.311	0.342/0.409	0.404/0.461	0.501/0.529	0.177/0.216	0.3/0.359
Four	0.28/0.327	0.352/0.397	0.092/0.264	0.29/0.327	0.382/0.463	0.433/0.496	0.507/0.553	0.196/0.222	0.317/0.375
Ten	0.290/0.336	0.355/0.403	0.106/0.281	0.299/0.339	0.407/0.491	0.438/0.504	0.514/0.56	0.209/0.233	0.327/0.393
Forty-one	0.325/0.375	0.396/0.447	0.116/0.322	0.331/0.372	0.467/0.549	0.509/0.57	0.566/0.595	0.24/0.264	0.369/0.437

* = very small eta, statistically insignificant.

1. *Source:* same as the preceding tables. Those tested were aged 20-21. Eta coefficients, analogous to correlations (see chapter IV). Computed according to 42 scales (series of exercises and questions). One only for basic spelling and grammar. Several of each of the other subjects in the table. For these subjects, the mean of eta is calculated according to various scales. For each entry, the eta to the left is calculated using only two levels: satisfactory and unsatisfactory. To the right, eta according to all levels in each scale (from 4 to 44 levels depending on the scale).

2. *Two categories:* working class and other. *Three categories:* working, middle and upper classes. *Eight categories:* unskilled and semi-skilled workers, skilled and highly skilled workers, foremen, white-collar employees, small businessmen and craftsmen, farmers, middle management, upper class. *Twenty-two categories:* agricultural employees, unskilled and semi-skilled workers, skilled workers, highly skilled workers, foremen, white collar employees, secondary school teachers, etc.

3. *Two levels:* 1. vocational qualification (non-manual trade) and higher qualifications; 2. vocational qualification (manual trade). *Three levels:* 1. no qualification; 2. vocational qualification; 3. secondary school qualification and analogous cases

(including university). *Four levels:* 1. no qualification; 2. vocational qualification (manual trade); 3. vocational qualification (non-manual trade); 4. secondary school qualification and analogous cases (including university). *Ten levels:* breakdown of those without a qualification according to the last level attended (primary, lower secondary, etc.); sub-division of the two types of vocational qualification in terms of whether they were obtained after an on-the-job apprenticeship with courses in a vocational school or after full-time studies in a vocational school, with, in addition, separation of vocational qualifications related to social work (and analogous cases). Separation of secondary school graduates (and analogous cases) and persons already enrolled at university. *Forty-one:* extreme degree of detail; five kinds of secondary high school qualification, plus primary school teacher's qualification, post-secondary technical qualifications, university degree, etc.

Table 31. Crude explanatory impact (maximum, minimum and mean) of the social background category and of the formal level of education. Young men. Switzerland (1984). According to Table 30[1]

	Crude explanatory impact (% of explained variance)	
	of the social background category	of the formal level of education
Maximum	14.4	35.4
Minimum	0.2	0.3
Mean[2]	3.3	11.5

1. Social background category, highest eta coefficient of Table 30 = 0.38, squared = 14.4%. The lowest, 0.039, squared = 0.2%, etc.
2. From eight eta coefficients shown in the column 'mean degree of dependence' in Table 30 with respect to the social background category and the ten eta coefficients given in the column in connection with the formal level of education.

Educational selection and social mobility

Two of the objectives of the educational process are especially difficult to reconcile: striving to overcome the many kinds of handicaps and forms of discrimination which adversely affect the studies of a number of pupils; and satisfying the need to orientate reasonable numbers of young people towards the types of activity available on the job market.

On one hand is the humanistic ideal of the best possible development of each and every individual as an end in itself; on the other is education as a means of preparing young people for the division of labour and the inequality of economic and social situations.

The problems to which this dilemma give rise have been abundantly investigated by educational sociologists and research specialists in social mobility.

These works have sought mainly to determine the extent to which attributes imposed at birth (for example, sex, the parental socio-economic status, the region of residence, etc.) influence education and, in conjunction with the latter, affect the career prospects of individuals. We are dealing here with aspects of the inequality of opportunity.

As the preceding chapters indicated, inequality of opportunity refers to the relationship between what individuals happen to receive at birth and what they subsequently achieve on their own, rightfully or otherwise (Dahrendorf, 1981). The distribution of occupations on the basis of imposed characteristics and schooling is not the only point to be considered by educational sociologists in this connection. They must also look into the inequality of opportunity of access to knowledge in terms of the education

Figure 11. Outline of influences (characteristics imposed at birth, education, occupational status)

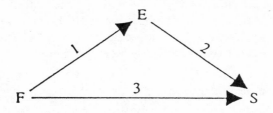

F = Fate, imposed characteristics: E = education, scholastic career, qualifications; S = occupational status.

---

received. Chapter II dealt with this aspect. The individual's access to political power, insofar as the latter influences the educational selection process, is a kindred problem.

Chapter VI will deal with the classical themes of the inequality of educational opportunity and its relationship to the distribution of occupations.

*　　*　　*

Numerous works have been devoted to individual facets of the question. In addition, studies have been carried out to examine the interrelationships between these various factors. Figure 11 gives an outline of them.

Segment 1 (F-E) corresponds to the problem of the inequality of educational opportunity. Segment 2 (E-S) corresponds to the relationship between the selection process within the education system and the distribution of jobs, at career start and later on. Segment 3 (F-S) corresponds to the question of the incidence of the parental social status on occupational and social status in adulthood; such is the object of the study of so-called 'between-generation' mobility (i.e. from one generation to the next). Social mobility also has 'within-generation' aspects: changes of occupational and social level in the course of one's career. Between-generation mobility and within-generation mobility are, of course, to be examined together, whenever this is possible. The latter causes the former to change as the individual grows older. Considered by itself, social mobility is not relevant to the problems of concern to educational sociology, except insofar as it has an impact on schooling. Hence, it is when analysing the relationships between the three segments mentioned above (F-E, F-S, E-S) that we will need to take up the question of social mobility, in combination with the inequality of educational opportunity and the latter's incidence on job allocation. We will concern ourselves only with between-generation mobility.

Inequality of educational opportunity

Ideas concerning the appropriate measures required to reduce the inequality of educational opportunity are evolving.

In the beginning, in the mid-nineteenth century, the emphasis was placed on making the quality of schools and curricula as equivalent as possible. In other words, the objective was limited to reducing the inequality of the instructional means made available to youngsters by the community. During the past several decades, the emphasis has shifted to the question of equalizing results. This led to attributing greater importance to measures - remedial instruction, in particular - which aimed at attenuating the disadvantages suffered by one category of pupils (Coleman, 1968).

Basically, the approach always aimed at modifying the means. But the new outlook goes further than the old. Rather than considering it sufficient to allow scholastic competition to occur - in principle - in the context of a more or less strictly partitioned education system - again, in principle -, it takes the handicaps of certain individuals more into account.

The results are of several kinds. First, formal results: scholastic success or failure in terms of grades, amount of grade repeating, distributions by section or college and, lastly, the level of education (diplomas) in the ordinary sense, namely that adopted by current educational statistics.

Next, real results: in particular, the effective supplement of knowledge and skills due to the education received. We will not deal with this question again (see Chapter II).

The incidence of schooling on the value of the professional situation attained is also to be counted among the real results, as is its effect on social mobility. These points will be examined in sections II and III of the present chapter.

*   *   *

Let us now consider the inequality of educational opportunity from the most common point of view (formal): access to the various levels and branches of education, diplomas obtained.

With respect to this question, abundant empirical data reveal two major trends which are so constant and so logical that they could almost be qualified as laws, if this notion is relevant to the social sciences.

A. The inequality of opportunity diminishes with economic and social development, and especially with the development of education systems.

B. At each phase of this development, inequality increases with level of education.

To identify these trends clearly, it is useful to compare periods which are not too close in time and countries which are not at similar stages of development.

To do the opposite, by considering things in detail, in the short term and on the basis of a single country or several countries at roughly the same stage of development, will often reveal very interesting situations, but it is difficult to distinguish the undercurrents of the evolution.

We will attempt here to pinpoint these undercurrents. They will be illustrated by means of six tables, relating to the incidence of several imposed traits. They are the sources of inequalities for different reasons.

1. *Sex.* Inequalities of this source do not spring from differences of standard of living or lifestyle. Girls and boys are distributed in the same proportions over all social categories. Differences of function and status between the masculine and feminine genders are the culprits.

2. *Social class*: working class, farmers, etc. Unlike the previous characteristic, this refers to strata within which the distribution according to income bracket and lifestyles differ.

3. *'Colour'*. This characteristic refers both to differences of standard of living and lifestyles and to outright discrimination.

4. *Period.* It is often forgotten, but few factors weigh as heavily in the balance of the destiny of individuals as the historical period in which they are chanced to be born. In the case of education alone, the inequality of the educational possibilities in any country will be considerable between, say, the generations who were aged from 5 to 20 between 1930 and 1945 and those who lived the same period of their

Table 32. School attendance. Major trends on a world-wide scale. A quarter of a century; 1960 & 1985[1]

School attendance rates by major kinds of region, according to age-group. In 1960 and 1985.

	Ages 6-11	Ages 12-17	Ages 18-23
Developed countries[2]			
1960	90.5	68.9	14.9
1985	90.9	86.3	32.7
	(1.004)[3]	(1.25)	(2.19)
Developing countries[4]			
1960	47.5	21.1	3.8
1985	72.7	46.0	13.7
	(1.53)	(2.18)	(3.61)
North America[5]			
1960	100	92.1	29.3
1985	100	99.5	50.7
	(1.00)	(1.08)	(1.73)
Africa (without the Arab countries)			
1960	29.6	17.1	1.4
1985	63.5	51.1	9.3
	(2.15)	(2.99)	(6.64)

1. *Unesco statistical yearbook*; 1985, table 2.11. Estimated percentage of the total numbers of each age group enrolled in schools (primary, secondary, technical and business schools, universities etc.)
2. Australia, Canada, Europe, Israel, Japan, New Zealand, USSR, United States and South Africa.
3. The figures in parentheses indicate the scope of progress between 1960 and 1985. Example: from 1960 to 1985, in developed countries, the percentage of 18-23-year-olds attending schools went from 14.9% to 32.7%, that is, the rate was more than doubled (32.7/14.9 = 2.19 times). A coefficient of 1 or around 1 indicates that there was no change or virtually no change.
4. The rest of the world, except for China and DPR Korea.
5. United States, Canada (plus the Bermuda Islands, Greenland, Saint-Pierre et Miquelon). The major regions concern North America and Africa (without the Arab countries) as contrasting examples. The Unesco *Yearbook* also singles out Europe (including the USSR), Asia, Oceania, Latin America and the Arab States.

lives between 1970 and 1985. In the intervening period, the organization and methods of education changed a great deal, and, under the impulse of evolution in the economy, mores and mentalities, and attitudes towards schools likewise changed.

5. *The country's degree of economic development.* For a given period, the educational possibilities and other factors differ depending on the country's position on the scale of economic development.

It would also be necessary to consider, among other things, inter-regional inequality: towns, proximate or remote rural areas, near-desert or mountainous regions, etc. This variable is one of the most powerful causes of educational inequality. Its incidence diminishes as the network of schools and channels of communication become more complete, at the same time as economic activities and ways of living and thinking change.

Major trend A: less inequality of opportunity as a function of development

This trend has a synchronic and a diachronic aspect. Examples of its synchronic aspect can be seen in Tables 32 and 34 by comparing, for a given year - 1960 or 1985 - developed and developing countries, or North America and Africa (excluding Arab countries).

In Table 32, various countries are, indeed, grouped into two large categories: developed and developing. Moreover, the table compares two regions of the world, the most developed (North America) and the least developed (Africa as a whole). It gives the school attendance rates according to age, in each of these regions of the world (percentage of children and young people from 6 to 11 years, 12 to 17 years, and 18 to 23 years, enrolled in educational institutions). This corresponds approximately to primary school, secondary school and types of training which follow, in particular, higher education.

Table 33 contains disparity rates: the chances of being enrolled in school in developed and developing countries, North America and Africa, according to age, in 1960 and in 1985. Table 34 deals with the inequality of chances of being enrolled in school according to sex for the same regions in the same years.

In 1960, as in 1985, the inequality of opportunity of access to schooling, according to age and sex, is all the greater as one descends the scale of development. This is a normal consequence of the difference in the amount of space available in the various categories of educational institution in comparison to the size of the age groups concerned, the state of transportation facilities, the intensity of motivation to attend school or university

Problems of sociology in education

Table 33. School attendance. Evolution of the degree of inequality between regions of the world: 1960 and 1985.[1] Disparity between developed and developing countries, North America and Africa: in 1960 and 1985.

Degree of inequality with respect to chances of attending school:

A. Between developed and developing countries

	Ages 6-11	Ages 12-17	Ages 18-23
1960	1.91	3.27	3.92
1985	1.25	1.88	2.39

B. Between North America and Africa (without the Arab States)

	Ages 6-11	Ages 12-17	Ages 18-23
1960	3.38	5.39	20.93
1985	1.57	2.63	5.45

1. As per table 32. Computed as follows, the school attendance rate in 1960 was, at age 6-11, 90.5% in developed countries and 47.5% in developing countries: 90.5/47.5 = 1.91 times greater, etc.

Table 34: School attendance. Evolution of inequality of opportunity between girls and boys. On a world-wide scale. A quarter of a century[1]

Region	Ages 6-11	Ages 12-17	Ages 18-23
Developed countries			
1960	1	1.05	1.57
1985	1	*1.01	1.04
Developing countries			
1960	1.51	1.90	2.80
1985	1.21	1.32	1.65
North America			
1960	1	1.01	1.41
1985	1	*1.01	*1.02
Africa (outside the Arab countries)			
1960	1.66	1.98	3.67
1985	1.17	1.42	2.33

* Girls have the advantage. Boys have the advantage in all other cases. 1 = same school attendance rate for both sexes.

1. Same source as for Table 32. In 1960, in developing countries, the school attendance rate of 6-11 year-old boys was 57.1% and that of girls 37.7%: 57.1/37.7 = 1.51 times greater, etc. The rates are not reproduced here. The table only provides ratios.

according to the economic, social and cultural context, and attitudes towards the education of girls versus boys.

* * *

Diachronic aspect: changes in the regions in Tables 32-34 between 1960 and 1985 and other changes according to two other examples. The first is that of the evolution which took place in the United States between 1940 and 1985, with regard to formal levels of education according to sex and 'colour' (Table 35). The second example is that of the evolution in France, from 1962 to 1980 with regard to access to university studies according to social background category (Table 36).

In the different examples cited, the inequality of opportunity shrank. This appears to be the general trend, with occasional blockages at a given level or in a given, specific category of institution. Social inequalities can change, and yet continue to exist. The inequalities which used to exist after the compulsory phase between pupils who were able to continue their studies and adolescents who joined the work force now occur at a later age, involving holders of secondary school qualifications versus vocational school graduates (Prost, 1986).

Major trend B: increase of inequality of opportunity with the raising of the level of education

The examples of Tables 32 to 35 and those of Table 36 illustrate this trend, which is also very general.

The last table indicates the distribution of secondary school students and students at university level according to the social category of their parents, in France, the USSR and in Poland during recent times. For France and Poland, it shows differences according to the type of section at the secondary level and the kind or level of university studies. With regard to Poland, data related to differences according to sex complement those related to social background.

At the various stages of the selection process the gaps widen. This is true of the distance separating young people of developed and developing countries, for the years 1960 and 1985. This is true of inequalities of opportunity based on 'race', in the United States in 1940 as well as in 1985. This is also true of the gap according to social background as shown in Table 37. This table further reflects the well-known fact that at a given level of studies, the gap according to social background is all the greater, the more prestigious the institution attended.

More refined analyses reveal the differences between first-class universities and other universities, etc. In certain countries, elite secondary schools and certain post-graduate 'Ivy League' or 'Oxbridge' universities serve particularly privileged circles and function as breeding grounds for top-level administrators, leaders of big business, some high-ranking military officers and the most coveted political posts.

The differences according to sex follow major trend B with, however, several nuances: in developed countries, girls tend to be better represented than boys at the secondary level, taken globally. They constitute a distinct majority in certain sections at this level. Naturally, the same applies to branches of higher education giving access to sectors of activity where graduates have the least difficulty finding jobs.

Gaps at a given point in time are explained by the state of social structures, the education system and mentalities. Major trend A is a consequence of the evolution of these parameters. It also has a simple mathematical aspect. In the case of major trend B, the mathematical aspect of the phenomena is particularly evident.

The more traditional a society is, the less the living conditions and the less the majority of families' perception of things will encourage them to send their children to school, particularly girls. Likewise, the cultural environment outside of school does not encourage many children from such backgrounds to succeed at school. In the least advanced societies, the school network is not dense. In many cases the distance to school is so great that it is often impossible to attend without leaving one's family. It may happen that the language spoken at home is not the same as that spoken in the classroom, which creates further difficulties. In these situations, the sum total of sociological hindrances, geographical obstacles and a more or less embryonic education system constitutes a severe handicap for large portions of the young population, girls in particular, from the point of view of school attendance and assimilation of curricula. These handicaps are attenuated with development.

In developed countries, the inequality of standards of living tends to make the degree of scholastic success vary more or less systematically according to social background category.

This inequality also tends to cause the interest in continuing in school, for a given level of scholastic achievement, to vary more or less systematically: for a good pupil aged 14-16 from an affluent background to embark upon a course of study of long duration entails only advantages and no disadvantages. Studies of this kind are, of course, tempting for a pupil of

Table 35. Evolution of the formal level of education by sex and 'colour'. United States: 1940 and 1985. Persons aged 25-19.[1]

	Complete secondary school studies		University studies	
	1940	1985	1940	1985
Population aged 25-29 years				
Men	36.0	85.9	6.9	23.1
Women	40.1	86.4	4.9	21.3
	(1.11)*[2]	(1.006)	(1.41)	(1.08)
'Whites'	41.2	86.8	6.4	23.2
'Blacks'	11.6	80.6	1.6	11.5
	(3.55)	(1.08)	(4.00)	(2.02)

* = girls fare better

1. Current population reports. Series P-20. No 415. Bureau of the Census, Washington, 123p. 1987. Complete secondary school studies: completed senior year (terminal level) of high school. Included are persons who later went on to post-secondary and university studies. University studies: four levels or more of college.

2. In 1940, young men had around 1.5 times (6.9/4.9 = 1.41) more chance of attending university than girls, etc.

---

the same capacity from an economically deprived background, but the extra lost time will need to be taken into account. In addition, failure to obtain the diploma involves the risk of entering the labour market in reduced circumstances. For a pupil of the same capacity from a privileged social background, this failure is easily surmountable with the help of the parents: he/she could turn to other studies, postponing even further the moment of entrance into the labour market, or take up a working course abroad, etc. These observations also apply to pupils whose performance at school is average or poor.

In developing countries, as elsewhere, but from a much higher threshold, these handicaps can be attenuated as the result of economic and social evolution, the diversification of curricula, and the improvement of educational practices. Against this background, other factors influencing access to schooling, such as sex and discrimination of a racial nature, come into play. Examples of this indicate that, in the United States, the modernization of society and of education tends to attenuate the effects of 'race'.

Such, in essence, are the genuine causes of major trend A.

Table 36. Evolution of the inequality of opportunity of pursuing university studies by social background category. France: 1959-1960 and 1981-1982

Male and female university students by social background category,[5] as %.

	W	A	M	U	X	Total
1959-1960[1]	4	6	53	33	5	100
1981-1982[2]	14	5	37	33	10	100

Distribution of men of around fifty according to social class[5]

	W	A	M	U	X	Total
1962[3]	39	20	30	7	4	100
1980[4]	46	9	31	12	2	100

Differences

	W	A	M	U
towards 1960	-9.75	-3.33	+1.77	+4.71
towards 1980	-3.29	-1.80	+1.19	+2.75

Reads as follows: for the children of blue-collar workers in 1960, the probability of attending university was around ten times less than would have been the case in a situation of equality of opportunity. In such a situation, these children would have represented 39% of the total student population. In real terms at the time, they represented 4%: 39% / 4% = 9.75 times less. Around twenty years later, the children of blue-collar workers were roughly three times (46 / 14 = 3.29 times) less likely to attend university than in a situation of equality.

1. Pascale Gruson & Janina Markiewicz, Lagneau (1983).
2. *Donneés sociales* (1984).
3. Men of between 45-54, working, Boudon (1973). It is assumed that they more or less represented the fathers of the students of the time.
4. Men of 40-49, working. *Donneés sociales* (1984).
5. w = working class (including service personnel); A = agriculture (farmers and agricultural workers); M = middle class (managers in the crafts, industry, retail trades, middle management, other white-collar workers); U = upper class (liberal professions and top management); X = miscellaneous.

Its mathematical explanation is that the lower the enrolment rate of a country or of a group at a given level the greater is the margin of potential progress and the less progress is required in order to reduce the gap in comparison with a given, more favoured, country or group. If the rates are high at the outset, potential progress is limited.

A progression of 5 points eclipses a departure percentage of 5%. The same progression in points hardly changes the magnitude of an initial percentage of 80%. The ratio between the new denominator (10%) and the new numerator (85%) nonetheless changes considerably: 80/5 = 16 times greater; 85/10 = 8.5 times greater.

The enrolment rate of the second country or social group in this imaginary example can again double, treble, etc. The other rate, meanwhile, is already close to the ceiling and cannot change radically.

This arithmetical mechanism tends to function for every change, no matter how small, occurring in change situations at the base of the pyramid, and not only in other parts of it.

Society being what it is at any given time, with the disparities it generates between social categories from the point of view of scholastic achievement and the balance between advantages/disadvantages conferred by the solutions which may be envisaged at each stage of the educational process, a somewhat analogous mathematical mechanism plays a fundamental role with regard to major trend B.

Let us imagine, borrowing from Boudon (*L'égalité des chances*, 1979; *La logique du social*, 1979), a classification of pupils into three social categories: A, B and C. The result of all of these factors is that, at each stage of the educational process, 80% of those in group A continue in the channels leading most directly to a university degree, the proportion of similar cases in group B is 75%, and in group C, 70%. These rather small differences tend to widen the gap in terms of equality of opportunity. Initially, each category comprised 1,000 individuals.

Stage I in Table 38 could be the separation into advanced and slow classes in primary school. Stages II-IV could correspond to streams at the compulsory secondary level and secondary school. Stages VI onwards could or could not lead to university admission, to the earning of a degree. The individuals in Group A have, in this fictitious example, almost three times a greater chance of obtaining a university degree than group C (2.90 times greater). At stage I, the gap was narrow (1.14). It grew gradually. The gap between groups A and B and between groups B and C also widened.

Inasmuch as any imposed trait (a region's or country's level of development, 'race', etc.) causes the allocation of young people to different streams at the crossing points in the education system to vary more or less systematically, it tends to make these gaps grow in proportion to the social background category. This is an arithmetic consequence of the fact that the selection process involves a series of steps and that, at each of these, the subsets under consideration tend to organize themselves in the same fashion with regard to the proportion of pupils being streamed into each branch.

Table 37. Distribution of pupils and students according to social background, at the outset (at the time of primary studies), at the time of secondary studies, and at the time of university studies, as well as the type of institution attended; France, the USSR and Poland circa 1980. With data concerning differences of orientation according to sex in Poland.

Country, levels, institutions	Distribution of pupils and students according to parents; social class					
I. France (circa 1975-1980)[1]	W	A	M	U	X	Total (%)
A. At the outset (all children of school age)	43	12	26	8	11	100
B. Secondary level, long census (towards age 16)	29	6	41	16	9	100
Which break down into:						
technical sections	39	6	38	8	10	100
literary sections	21	6	40	25	8	100
C. University						
University studies, bachelor level (around age 19-20)	17	6	39	29	9	100
University studies, master level	12	6	36	38	8	100
University studies, doctoral level	8	5	34	41	12	100
II. USSR (circa 1975-1978)[2]	W	A	O			Total (%)
A. At the outset (beginning of primary school studies)	58	16	26			100
B. Secondary school level, general studies (complete secondary school education, at around 17 years)	50	14	36			100
C. Full-time university studies, 1st year (at around 19-20 years)	46	8	47			100

III. Poland (circa 1975-1976)[3]	W	A	O	Total (%)
A. At the outset (end of primary studies)	44	30	26	100
B. Secondary level vocational schools (short-term training, at around 16 years)	58	26	16	100
Vocational schools (long-term programme, at around 16 years)	43	21	37	100
High school, at around 16 years	35	16	50	100
C. Higher education. Admitted to universities, all institutions combined (at around 19-20 years)	32	10	58	100
Which breaks down into:				
normal schools	41	12	47	100
universities	33	9	58	100
schools of engineering	30	7	63	100
medical schools	25	8	68	100

	Orientation according to sex		Total (%)
	Girls	Boys	
A. At the outset (end of primary studies)	50.2	49.8	100
B. Secondary level vocational schools (short-term training, at around 16 years)	39	61	100
Vocational schools (long-term programme, at around 16 years)	55	45	100
High school, at around 16	71	29	100
C. Higher education. Admitted to universities, all institutions combined (at around 19-20 years)	52	48	100
Which breaks down into:			
normal schools	75	25	100
universities	66.5	33.5	100
schools of engineering	29	72	100
medical schools	65	35	100

1. France. Selected data from various tables from *Donneés sociales* (1981). Parents' social class: W = working class (including service personnel); a = agriculture (farmers and agricultural workers); M = middle class (managers in the crafts, industry, retail trades, middle management, other white-collar workers). U = upper class (liberal professions and top management); X = miscellaneous.

2. According to a study in Russian (*The school of higher learning, factor of structural change in the developed socialist society*). Moscow, 1978, quoted by Gruson, Pascale, and Markiewicz-Lagneau, Janina (1983): W = working class; A = agriculture (persons on collective farms); O = others (white-collar workers and specialists).

3. Study by J. Bialecki, in Polish (*The choice of school and reproduction of social structure*, 1982), quoted by P. Gruson and J. Markiewicz-Lagneau in the above-mentioned work: W = working class; A = agriculture; O = others (non-manual workers).

Table 38. Number of young people currently in programmes leading the most directly to a university degree[1]

		Stages of schooling							
category	Starting	I	II	III	IV	V	VI	VII	Degree
A	1000	800	640	512	410	328	262	210	168
B	1000	750	563	422	317	238	179	134	101
C	1000	700	490	343	240	168	118	83	58

	Degree of inequality[2]							
category	I	II	III	IV	V	VI	VII	Degree
A	1.14	1.31	1.49	1.71	1.95	2.22	2.53	2.90
B	1.07	1.15	1.23	1.32	1.42	1.52	1.61	1.74
C	1	1	1	1	1	1	1	1

1. Assumptions: that each category numbers 1,000 individuals to begin with. At each stage 80% of A, 75% of B and 70% of C remain on the courses leading directly to higher education (the same percentages apply to stage VII to the degree).

2. 800 per thousand/700 per thousand = 1.14 times more; 750 per thousand/700 per thousand = 1.07 times more, etc.

In reality, the effects of this basic mechanism are felt in various ways, according to the economic and social context, mentality (in particular, attitudes towards education, the aspirations of pupils), the number and nature of forms of education (and vocational training) which the education system offers at each stage, the content of curricula, teaching methods, the criteria for evaluating the work of pupils, the formal rules and practices with regard to admissions, study grant policies, etc.

*   *   *

Theories put forward on the subject of inequality in educational opportunity abound (Hurn, 1978). They differ from each other in terms of the weight they assign to various categories of factors involved, in particular:

I. Contextual factors (society)

(a) *The economy.* Relationships between the structure (sections, etc.) and functioning (methods, practices, etc.) of the education system, the division of labour, the state of the labour market, the future outlook in this regard.

(b) *Social stratification.* Inequality of incomes, of living conditions. Differences in lifestyles: social classes, ethnic groups, regions, castes.

(c) *Mentality, culture.* The country's traditions: beliefs, customs, cultural distances: language of the classroom and the languages of diverse segments of the population.

(d) *Social roles (sex), discrimination* ('race', native citizens, foreigners according to country of origin). Favourable and unfavourable prejudices.

(e) *Geography, communication.* Towns versus rural areas, isolated regions.

II. Contextual factors (family, particular background)

(f) *Family.* Distribution of authority within the household. Emotional relationships. Divorce, separation of parents. Children living without parents. Family traditions. Resources.

(g) *Social sub-classes,* particular backgrounds, specifically, very privileged or very underprivileged. Shanty towns. 'Fourth World'. Slums. Agrarian or other sub-proletariats.

III. Education, educators

(h) *Structure,* kinds of schools, sections, colleges, vocational training centres. Number. Explicit objectives. De facto functions.

(i) *Resources*, equipment, personnel in the different types of schools, etc. Teacher salaries. Teachers' training.

(j) *Methods and curricula*. Textbooks. Teaching methods. Manner of evaluating the pupils' work. Admission criteria. Official aspect of evaluation and admission standards, unofficial practices. Degree of compatibility of educational content and teaching methods with living conditions, ways of thinking, conceptual references, Weltanschauung, the way of saying things, etc., of certain categories of pupils and of parents. Educational code of perception and code of conduct and code familiar to pupils. Perverse effects of the selection process and of the extension of the average duration of schooling: more severe and longer competition, tending in reality to exert an earlier influence; the predominant concern becoming that of rank to the detriment of personal development carried out at individual speeds and in keeping with personal foci of interest; increase in the number of those disappointed, of frustrations and stress; tension within the family; confusion among teachers. Often a professional level which is no better or even poorer after a greater number of years of schooling and more exams.

(k) *Attitudes of teachers*. Particularly towards disadvantaged pupils.

(l) *Remedial programmes*.

IV. *Pupils*

(m) *Motivation, aptitude*. Unequal distribution according to major social categories, region, sub-classes, particular backgrounds, ethnic groups, sex, etc. Cerebral development (inexhaustible and obscure quarrel about hereditary and other factors affecting IQs). Emotional handicaps. Behavioural disorders.

(n) *Microsociology*, ethnology, social psychology of educational relationships (teacher/pupil). Pupil/pupil relationships ('peers'). Youth culture with its variants, some rather fostering deviant behaviour and adjustment to failure, others encouraging integration, work and scholastic achievement. Problem of the internalization of scholastic failure in the form of a feeling of definitive, general inferiority. The opposite for the internalization of scholastic achievement as a guarantee of superiority in everything and a vocation as a leader, as one of the privileged.

V. Models, simulation

(o) *Elucidation of the mathematical effects* of the conditions in which decisions are made (by families, schools or even the pupils themselves) which lead to the way in which the breakdown of pupils into sections at the various stages of schooling is structured, and the structure of the distribution of young people by category of diploma (formal level of instruction). Works by Boudon, in particular.

*   *   *

A few titles have already been mentioned in the preceding chapters, in the discussion concerning the difference between the problem of inequality of real knowledge and that of formal aspects of educational inequality. They will not be quoted again here. Let us mention several other important works on the inequality of opportunity with respect to schooling: Boudon (1979), Bowles & Gintis (1976), Carnoy & Levin (1976), Cherkaoui (1979), Coleman (1966 and 1968), Dahrendorf (1981), Halsley (1980), Hurn (1978), Jencks (1972), Husén (1978 and 1979), Parsons (1951 and other works) and Young (1961).

Formal level of education and occupational status

The distribution of individuals according to the nature and level of schooling they attained has a major impact on their distribution by occupation. Yet the degree of correspondence between type of diploma (or lack of diploma) and kind of occupation is far from being strictly predictable, for a variety of reasons.

To begin with, economic and demographic reasons. Others reasons are related to the structure of outputs emanating from the education system. Still others relate to the role which regulations and custom attribute to diplomas as such, when hiring someone for their first job and during the subsequent stages of their working career, in addition to the role of effective skills and other characteristics of applicants.

All the parameters of the relationship between formal level of education and occupation are in evolution. It is thus in a changing economic and social framework that individual careers develop, with the mobility (changes of post, grade, company, sector) which this entails. For a given generation, what changes least is the breakdown of its members in terms of formal level of education. However, some individuals acquire new qualifications after the completion of their initial schooling, by enrolling in university continuing education programmes, courses for staff organized by companies, administrations, etc.

*   *   *

The activities in which one can engage in a country depend on the state of its *economy*. To be sure, the real training of individuals is one of the factors of economic dynamism: insofar as the population possesses the skills required, it will be possible for it to undertake, innovate and develop, on condition, however, that the necessary investments are available and that the country is not paralysed because of oppression or for other reasons. An insufficiently skilled population is doomed to stagnation in any case, even if investment is set aside and the most ingenious development schemes are put forward.

It remains that, sector by sector, region by region, business by business, the economic system - where careers commence and develop - is the source of a given demand for labour. At the same time, it excludes all activities exceeding that demand, or dooms them to failure if they are undertaken - unless they are subsidized at a loss.

In a given economic climate the relation between supply and demand is affected by the volume of the available active population, after adjustment for the rate of activity by age and sex (Sauvy, 1976; Vimont, 1981). This is the *demographic* aspect of the problem.

The rate of women's involvement in activity tends to increase. This, on the positive side, increases the supply of labour to be optimally exploited. But, on the negative side, this also increases the difficulties to be surmounted to place the holders of certain diplomas in jobs suited to them or to avoid unemployment.

The number of younger people who are entering the job market fluctuates according to the birth rate, the youth mortality rate, migrations. In developing countries, this volume is experiencing rapid or even explosive growth. In developed countries, now that the wave of the baby boom generation which entered the labour market approximately from 1965 to 1985 has passed, the contingent of young people to be integrated into the economy has tended to decrease.

The outputs emanating from the education system act on the structure of the job supply. The imbalance is often considerable between the distribution of young people by kind of training and the demand: large surpluses of graduates in certain sectors and at certain levels, insufficient supply elsewhere.

The shortage of graduates thus affecting certain sectors results in relying on candidates with diverse types of educational background, often inferior to those which had been demanded earlier, in order to fill the available posts as well as possible. Surpluses have the opposite effect. They tend to oblige the excess of diploma holders in the specialization they were trained for to find work elsewhere, as best they can.

Moreover, the *standards and customs* regulating access to various types of posts vary considerably according to country and to sector.

In some sectors, explicit standards, established by law, as well as regulations adopted by professions, administrations and businesses, define the diplomas required. These norms are more or less limitative. They are enforced with varying degrees of strictness. They are proper to the public administration, liberal and intellectual professions - teaching is a typical example - for certain sectors of social work, the offices and laboratories of many large businesses, of various manual or technical trades more or less organized into guilds (Caplow, 1985).

In very broad sectors of the economy, the formal level of education plays no role whatsoever, nor even an accessory role, especially after several years' experience.

In any case, qualifications are rarely the sole determinant in the decision to award a salaried position, either as first employment, or later on when a promotion is being offered, for example. The influence they exert with regard to non-salaried activities is extremely vague.

With regard to salaried positions, actual skills are taken as much into consideration, and normally more so, than diplomas. Personality also counts a great deal.

Recommendations and criticisms have an influence, contacts can play a role, as well as purely personal favouritism and its opposite as well. All of this against a backdrop of practices shaped by preferences and discrimina-tions, generally unacknowledged, pertaining to age, sex, religion, opinions, 'colour', social background, personal lifestyle, appearance, etc.

These practices not only affect decisions concerning workers. They also influence authorizations and loans granted to self-employed persons and even the size of their clientele.

They influence the professional aspirations of individuals, too. The activities they strive after tend to be a function of what they feel is compatible with their abilities, their qualifications and their social background. For the same motives, individuals may rule out other jobs.

Even in the most tightly regulated professions, it is relatively rare that only one kind of qualification gives access to a specific type of job. Most of the time, several kinds of qualification are suitable: for a given civil service position, for example, a liberal arts degree, a degree in law, economics, mathematics, in short, any university degree whatsoever, not to mention technical or commercial school qualifications, could be suitable.

Moreover, many businesses and administrations offer in-house staff refresher and promotion programmes. Their objective is, in particular, to help persons who have no qualification, or a not very suitable qualification at the outset, to attain management positions.

In many sectors, automatic promotion based on seniority is still another factor influencing the relationship between formal level of education and the post held.

In general, concerning professions in trade, industry and many other sectors requiring few qualifications, no explicit norm exists yet or the qualifications are still vague. Custom is usually the only point of reference, applying in varying sets of circumstances (for example, the absolute necessity or not of filling a post) to candidates who display equally varying sets of characteristics (skills, sex, background, etc.).

The state of the relationship schooling/occupation is, therefore, at the level of a country or region, the result of the action of a great number of factors.

The situation can be analysed by means of more or less detailed classifications. The ideal would be to have an ultra-precise nomenclature for qualifications. The names would indicate the nature and exact level of the educational programmes followed. This is what the university services attempt to do when establishing the degree of equivalency for the qualifications of students wishing to enrol. In addition, it would be necessary to be more detailed with regard to the evaluation of the level of professional activities. To do this, it would be necessary to take into account not only salary, but also job security, degree of freedom at work, the complexity of tasks, the social prestige of the profession, advancement possibilities, insurance, and amount of pension.

For comparisons over time, it would be desirable to have equally minute classifications for each period under consideration.

Some censuses, without going quite this far, provided rather precise indications concerning the type of qualification according to the profession exercised, which is also relatively well-defined.

These indications show that, in general, people often work outside the field for which they were trained. Doctors are virtually the only group of individuals to be practically all involved in the profession for which they were trained and for which they have a monopoly in its exercise. Many law degree holders do not enter the legal profession, or if they do, do not remain there. They find employment in sectors outside the legal profession, in civil service, commercial and communications jobs. Likewise, to give another example, many persons trained as engineers turn, either immediately after training or later on in their careers, to business or to other sectors outside of their trade: they become administrative employees, salespeople, etc. Similar observations can be made concerning the majority of other categories of qualification.

It should be noted, meanwhile, that, fortunately, most schools, apprenticeship programmes and colleges do not seek to prepare young people for a single, narrowly defined form of professional activity. On the contrary, their goal is to make them capable of taking advantage of different opportunities, of adapting accordingly, of improving their skills, of retraining if necessary.

The tables in which individuals are separated into several levels of formal education and several main socio-professional categories reflect these facts, but do not account for individual cases.

They show that the spread of graduates of any formal level of education by socio-professional category is generally rather large. But, of course, they also show that, depending on their formal level of education and allowing for exceptions, these individuals occupy a given part of the pyramid of socio-professional categories, some higher, some lower. The career opportunities available to them are thus diverse (holders of the same qualification are split up among several occupational categories), but not equivalent (they are not distributed equally among the different levels of the pyramid).

In short, formal levels of education constitute statistical strata (see preceding chapters) from the point of view of the distribution of their members by type of occupation. The correlations translating the overall degree of inter-relatedness between the two - formal level of education, kind of occupation - can vary a great deal from one country to another. In different Western countries, the classifications involving a limited number of formal levels of education and of social categories produce correlations for men aged 21 to 65 years (1974-1976) ranging from .300 to .500 in magnitude (Girod, 1984). Certain Scandinavian studies - restricted to wage-earners holding steady jobs and to small samples - resulted in exceptional correla-

Table 39. Formal level of education and socio-professional category (according to occupation): correlation. Three countries[1]

	Men	Women
France (1970), ages 16-52)[1]	0.537	0.668
United Kingdom (1972, ages 25-39)[1]	0.520	
United States (1962, ages 20-64)[1]	0.596	
United States (ages 25-44)		
1950	0.542	0.612
1985	0.574	0.548

1. Correlations calculated by assigning numerical values to formal levels of education and socio-professional categories and ranking them from highest to lowest, by: T. Tachibanaki (France, documentation generously made available by the Institut national de la statistique et des études économiques, eight formal levels of education, twenty seven socio-professional categories; A H Halsey (United Kingdom, in Karabel & Halsey, 1977, five formal levels of education, detailed scale of socio-professional categories); Blau & Duncan, 1967 (United States, nine formal levels of education, detailed scale of socio-professional categories).
2. Based on information used for tables 43 to 45. The four formal levels of education of these tables are numbered in the order in which they figure in these tables. The same applies to the six socio-professional categories.

---

tions, considerably higher, attaining about .800 (Pontinen & Uusitalo, 1975). Let us nonetheless take note of this special case.

Admittedly, the real situations are probably rather diverse: ranging from countries in which in-house apprenticeship programmes and job performance or even family relations predominate, to countries in which training takes place essentially in the classroom and qualifications confer the right to occupy a given type of post. It must also be acknowledged that as long as it has not been possible to adopt international agreements with regard to classifications, the variety of qualifications will cause the results to vary more or less artificially. Efforts are being made to remedy this.

The examples given in Table 39 can no doubt be considered quite typical of the most common correlations obtained on the basis of classifications which are already rather detailed. The correlations of this table range from just over 0.5 to nearly 0.7. Such correlations indicate that, on average, the socio-professional level is explained by the formal level of education to a proportion of between one-quarter and one-half. This involves the crude impact of the latter variable, that is, the influence of all characteristics (social background, in particular) which are more or less systematically linked to it. On the basis of these indications, therefore, the socio-professional classification depends 50% or more on causes which are independent of the formal level of education.

*   *   *

An identical correlation obtained for two countries or at two different times in a single country indicates that in either case the variables under consideration are linked to the same degree. But the distribution of individuals according to the levels of each of these variables can vary a great deal, just as their distribution among the cells resulting from the cross-tabulation of these variables can vary considerably: the best-off (at the top of the classification according to either variable), the least-favoured (at the very bottom on either side), intermediary groups.

We will now examine this point more closely taking, as an example, the United States. The distribution by type of case has changed a great deal in that country, while the correlations formal level of education/kind of occupation have remained relatively constant.

Two periods will be considered: 1950 and 1985. The observation will concern generations who were aged 25 to 44 years at each of these dates.

The case of the 25-44 year olds of 1950 takes us back to American society in the first half of the twentieth century. The members of this generation were born between 1906 and 1925. They were educated in the framework of the successive forms of the education system in the United States from around 1910 to 1945. The oldest individuals joined the work force towards 1925. The others followed until 1940-1950. This was a difficult period, except, perhaps towards the very end.

The '25-44 year olds' of 1985 were better-off. They were born between 1941 and 1960. Their schooling took place between 1946 and 1980 approximately. They joined the labour force over a period ranging from 1960 to around 1975-1985. Their trajectory, therefore, is situated in the second half of this century. It corresponds in large part to years of exceptional development, more sluggish towards the end.

Judging by the correlations of Table 39 alone, one could be tempted to conclude that the relationship formal level of education/socio-professional category changed little between 1950 and 1985 in the case of these generations. But after examining what these correlations conceal, very large differences appear.

We should begin by pointing out that the volume of the working population practically doubled: 61 million workers in 1950, 107 million in 1985.

Table 40. Evolution of the size of the active population aged 25-44 (in millions)

	1950	1985	Difference
Men	19	31	+12
Women	7	24	+17
Total	26	55	+29

This increase is due in a large measure to the increased participation of women. One out of three women were working in 1950. In 1985, the proportion had risen to more than one in two. Because of this, in 1985 there were 30 million women more in the working population than in 1950. With regard to men, the number of those working in 1985 was 18 million more than in 1950.

The number of workers aged 25-44, meanwhile, evolved as shown in Table 40 (in millions).

It is thus within an expanding labour market that the careers of the generations in question began and developed. These very generations were comprised of a greater number of individuals requiring jobs, especially women. These changes of size and composition according to sex were compounded by a radical recomposition of the formal education pyramid and of occupations.

From the point of view of completed education, the distribution has shifted considerably upwards. The most common case (Table 43, column marked 'Total') was in 1954, and concerns the 'no qualification' group. In 1985, only a small minority remained at this level. The most frequently encountered case became that of persons having completed their studies in post-secondary institutions.

The distribution of jobs has also shifted upwards (Table 45, row labelled 'Total'). This shift, however, was not as radical as that of formal levels of education.

The direction of evolution for these two structures is thus the same: ascendant. But the pace of this evolution is faster for levels of education than for socio-professional categories as the growth (+ sign) and decline (- sign) coefficients indicate.

With respect to the classifications of Tables 41-45, it is to be expected that, logically:

1. The formal level of education of the members of various socio-professional categories tended to *rise*.

2. The level of the jobs obtained by the holders of various formal levels of education tended to *decline*.

The changes which effectively occurred, however, were not mechanically dictated by the pace with which these two structures evolved.

Trends 1 and 2 above indicate the general direction of the modifications which were to be expected. They leave room for various possibilities. The holders of university degrees, for instance, might have continued to retain more or less posts at the top of the socio-professional pyramid, etc.

Moreover, those making up the categories defined by the formal level of education and that of the professional groups are heterogeneous and changing. The schooling corresponding to each formal level has changed. The same applies to the nature of the economic and social activities and situations combined in each socio-professional category. Only the name of the category remains constant.

Indeed, these sets include a variety of cases. Secondary and post-secondary schools, as well as universities, offer extremely varied programmes, in the United States in particular. They range from literary and scientific programmes to training in all sorts of trades for industry, commerce, the administration, the crafts, agriculture, not to mention careers in communications and the arts.

The higher the percentage of young people attending institutes of higher education, the more diversified the programmes offered by these institutions. Their goals differ to the same extent. This evolution more or less keeps pace with that of the labour market.

In addition, professions change. The nature of the tasks corresponding to each of them also changes. Working conditions, salaries and lifestyles of the members in various professions evolve.

Farmers nowadays only bear a rather remote resemblance to farmers of the past, for example. New specialities have made their way into agriculture or are at present of greater importance in that field than previously; agricultural techniques are no longer the same as in the past; agricultural production in all its forms has become increasingly automated; computerized management practices have become more widespread; farmers' dwellings have been modernized and the standard of living of most of them has improved.

Table 41. Formal level of education and socio-professional category (according to occupation), United States: 1950 and 1985. By sex. Persons aged 25-44. Frequencies as a percentage[1]

Men (1950): socio-professional category (N = 19 million)

Formal level of education	Unskilled, semi-skilled, and analogous workers	Craftsmen skilled workers foremen	Farmers	Clerks, sales personnel	Business management	Intellectual, technical, and related professions	Total (%)
No qualification	28.7	12.7	6.9	4.2	3.7	0.8	57.0
Secondary qualification	7.5	6.1	1.7	5.2	3.5	1.5	25.5
Short-term post-secondary education	1.3	1.2	0.3	2.3	1.8	1.5	8.4
University	0.4	0.4	0.2	1.5	1.5	5.1	9.1
Total (as a percentage)	37.9	20.4	9.1	13.2	10.5	8.9	100

Men (1985): socio-professional category (N = 31 million)

Formal level of education	Unskilled, semi-skilled, and analogous workers	Craftsmen skilled workers foremen	Farmers	Clerks, sales personnel	Business management	Intellectual, technical, and related professions	Total (%)
No qualification	6.4	3.9	0.7	0.9	0.4	0.2	12.5
Secondary qualification	13.9	11.5	1.3	5.2	3.0	1.7	36.6
Short-term post-secondary education	5.2	4.8	0.5	4.7	3.0	2.9	21.1
University	1.9	1.6	0.5	5.5	7.9	12.4	29.8
Total (as a percentage)	27.4	21.8	3.0	16.3	14.3	17.2	100

Women (1950): socio-professional category (N = 7 million)

Formal level of education	Unskilled, semi-skilled, and analogous workers	Craftsmen skilled workers foremen	Farmers	Clerks, sales personnel	Business management	Intellectual, technical, and related professions	Total (%)
No qualification	34.8	1.0	0.4	9.6	1.7	0.9	48.4
Secondary qualification	9.1	0.5	0.1	18.7	1.7	2.2	32.3
Short-term post-secondary education	1.2	0.1	*	4.9	0.6	3.5	10.3
University	0.3	*	*	1.9	0.3	6.4	8.9
Total (as a percentage)	45.4	1.6	0.5	35.1	4.3	13.0	100

Women (1985): socio-professional category (N = 24 million)

Formal level of education	Unskilled, semi-skilled, and analogous workers	Craftsmen skilled workers foremen	Farmers	Clerks, sales personnel	Business management	Intellectual, technical, and related professions	Total (%)
No qualification	6.2	0.4	0.2	2.0	0.2	0.2	9.2
Secondary qualification	12.9	1.4	0.4	21.5	3.2	2.7	42.1
Short-term post-secondary education	3.2	0.3	0.2	11.2	2.9	4.6	22.4
University	1.0	0.3	0.1	5.8	4.4	14.7	26.3
Total (as a percentage)	23.3	2.4	0.9	40.5	10.7	22.2	100

* = less than 0.05%

1. USA. Bureau of the Census, 1950, *US census of population: education, special reports*, P-E, No 5B. Washington, 129 pages, 1953. For 1985: *Educational attainment in the United States: March 1972 to 1985*. Current population series P-20, No 415, Bureau of the Census, Washington, 123 pages, 1987.

No qualification: three years of high school at most; *high school qualification*: the fourth and last year of high school; *short-term post-secondary education*: 1-3 years of college; *University*: 4 years or more of college.

Intellectual, technical and related professions; from primary school teacher, social worker, technician, librarian, broadcaster, to the highest liberal, scientific, technical, and artistic professions; *business, management*: heads of businesses, managers, business administrators, professional level civil servants; *clerks, sales personnel*: secretaries, accountants, typists, salespersons; *farmers*: 1950, only those self-employed, in 1985, including agricultural labourers; *craftsmen, skilled workers, foremen*: bakers, mechanics, electricians, tailors etc. whether self-employed or not, railroad engineers, for example; *unskilled, semi-skilled and analogous workers*: the remainder of the working population; semi-qualified workers in industry, servers, lorry drivers, firemen, elevator attendants, labourers, traffic policemen, etc.

This table includes persons (aged 25-44) involved in an occupation (according to which they are classified).

Table 42. Pace of evolution (from 1950 to 1985)[1]

	Men	Women
No qualification	-4.5	-5.3
Unskilled and semi-skilled and analogous workers	-1.4	-1.9
Secondary school diploma	+1.4	+1.3
Craftsmen, skilled workers, foremen	+1.1	+1.4
Farmers	-3.0	+1.8
Short-term post-secondary school studies	+2.5	+2.2
Clerks, sales personnel	+1.2	+1.2
Business, managers	+1.4	+2.5
University	+3.3	+2.9
Intellectual, technical and related professions	+1.9	+1.7

1. As per table 41, read as follows: from 1960 to 1985, the proportion of male 'non-qualifi-
cation holders' went from 56.85% to 12.5%; thus decreasing by a factor of 4.5. In the case
of women, the proportion of intellectual and related professions went from 13.05 in 1960
to 22.2% in 1985. It thus nearly doubled (+1.7 times, to be precise).

The schoolmaster and schoolmistress have to deal with problems which differ to some extent from those they had to confront in the past. Their social status has changed considerably. Such observations hold true for nearly all professions.

This is a far cry from the ideal analyses mentioned earlier which would ascertain the relationship between training and precisely graded occupational situations for each period.

Our tables simply break the population down into several kinds of training background and professional activities. What is clearest with respect to formal levels of education is that they generally correspond to different numbers of years of schooling: 12 for secondary school graduates; 13-15 for short-term higher level education; 16 and more for the individuals listed under 'University'.

The socio-professional categories in our tables include occupations which range from the least sought after to the most prestigious. But this concerns the mean value for various professions. In each category, certain professions deviate considerably from this mean (Treiman, 1977).

Table 43. Formal level of education by socio-professional category (according to occupation). United States: 1950 and 1985. By sex. Ages 25.44. As %[1]

Formal level of education	Socio-professional category												
	Unskilled, semiskilled and and similar cases		Craftsmen, skilled workers, foremen		Farmers		Clerks, sales personnel		Businessmen, managers		Intellectual, technical and related professions		Total (%)	
	1950	1985	1950	1985	1950	1985	1950	1985	1950	1985	1950	1985	1950	1985
Men														
No qualification	75.6	23.6	62.1	17.7	75.6	24.6	31.7	5.5	34.8	3.0	9.1	0.9	56.8	12.5
High school qualification	19.9	50.7	30.0	52.8	19.1	43.7	39.6	31.8	33.5	20.7	16.4	10.1	25.6	36.6
Short post-secondary studies	3.4	18.8	5.9	22.1	3.7	16.7	17.7	29.0	17.4	21.1	16.9	16.8	8.5	21.1
University	1.0	6.9	2.0	7.4	1.6	15.1	10.9	33.8	14.3	55.2	57.6	72.3	9.0	29.8
Total (%)	100	100	100	100	100	100	100	100	100	100	100	100	100	100
Women														
No qualification	76.6	26.4	61.6	17.9	75.6	18.1	27.4	5.0	39.3	2.1	6.6	0.8	48.4	9.2
High school qualification	20.0	55.3	30.2	58.6	16.0	44.2	53.4	53.1	39.2	30.0	17.2	12.2	32.3	42.1
Short post-secondary studies	2.6	13.8	5.4	12.9	5.0	21.9	13.9	27.6	13.5	26.9	26.8	20.7	10.3	22.4
University	0.8	4.4	2.8	10.6	3.4	15.8	5.3	14.3	7.9	41.0	49.4	66.2	9.0	26.3
Total (%)	100	100	100	100	100	100	100	100	100	100	100	100	100	100

1. Same source, same classification as Table 41.

Table 44. *Level of instruction and socio-professional category. Evolution of various combinations. United States: 1950 and 1985. According to sex. Ages 25-44. Percentages*[1]

	Men		Women	
Combinations	1950	1985	1950	1985
'Traditional' combinations[2]	48.3	11.0	36.2	6.8
'Modern' combinations[3]	13.7	36.4	17.6	43.6
Other	38.0	52.6	46.1	49.6
Total (%)	100	100	100	100

1. As per table 41.
2. No qualification/manual trade (unskilled or semi-skilled, plus craftsmen, farmers).
3. Short-term post-secondary studies or university/non-manual trade beginning with clerks, salesperson).

The data which will be examined thus reflect only the extent to which, on average, the respective socio-professional category tends to depend on the formal level of education, or, if one prefers, on the number of years spent within the education system. It is hardly possible to go any further, given the documentation currently available.

Table 41 gives an overview of the distribution both with regard to formal level of education and the socio-professional category.

It is on the basis of such two-way distributions that the correlations quoted above are calculated. They do not tell us anything about the distribution of individuals according to the cells in the grid, in other words, according to the combined disadvantage of a low formal level of education and unskilled employment, according to the intermediate combinations (poor on one side, average on the other, etc.) and according to the most favourable combinations (high, high). This distribution has changed considerably in an upward direction. The outlook which this table presents gives a positive interpretation of the facts, one of an upward progression.

The indications which follow describe in outline form the movement observed when the combinations are reduced to three types only: 'traditional', 'intermediate' and 'modern'.

In the combinations labelled 'traditional' in Table 44, lack of a qualification is coupled with the exercise of a manual trade. The so-called 'modern'

Table 45: *Socio-professional category in terms of occupation by formal level of education. United States: 1950 and 1985. By sex. Persons aged 25-44. As a percentage.*

Formal level of education	Unskilled, semiskilled and similar cases	Craftsmen, skilled workers, foremen	Farmers	Clerks, sales personnel	Businessmen, managers	Intellectual, technical and related professions	Total (%)
Men							
No qualification							
1950	50.4	22.2	12.1	7.4	6.5	1.4	100
1985	51.6	30.8	5.9	7.1	3.4	1.2	100
High school qualification							
1950	29.4	23.8	6.8	20.4	13.8	5.7	100
1985	37.9	31.5	3.6	14.2	8.1	4.7	100
Short-term post-secondary education							
1950	15.1	14.2	3.9	27.5	21.6	17.7	100
1985	24.4	22.9	2.4	22.4	14.4	13.6	100
University							
1950	4.4	4.4	1.6	16.0	16.7	56.8	100
1985	6.3	5.5	1.5	18.5	16.6	41.6	100
Total							
1950	37.9	20.4	9.1	13.2	10.5	8.9	100
1985	27.4	21.8	3.0	16.3	14.4	17.1	100
Women							
No qualification							
1950	72.2	2.2	0.8	19.9	3.4	1.8	100
1985	67.1	4.6	1.7	22.1	2.5	2.0	100
High school qualification							
1950	28.1	1.6	0.2	58.0	5.1	6.9	100
1985	30.7	3.3	0.9	51.1	7.6	6.4	100
Short-term post-secondary education							
1950	11.8	0.9	0.2	47.5	5.6	34.0	100
1985	14.4	1.4	0.9	50.1	12.7	20.5	100
University							
1950	3.8	0.5	0.2	20.6	3.7	71.1	100
1985	4.0	0.9	0.5	22.0	16.6	56.0	100
Total							
1950	45.5	1.7	0.5	35.1	4.2	13.0	100
1985	23.4	2.4	0.9	40.6	10.6	22.2	100

combinations associate a higher level of education with a non-manual occupation. The remaining combinations are intermediate.

The proportion of 'traditional' combinations has dropped drastically, that of 'intermediate' combinations has increased. That of the 'modern' combinations has increased even more. Table 41 presents these combinations in greater detail.

The outlook presented by Table 43 is also positive. It indicates an elevation of the formal level of education of members of the various socio-professional categories. In the same way as these individuals have, in general, greater access to comfort, to medical care, etc., they also have greater access to means of instruction. Individuals in the manual trades, even trades requiring few or no qualifications, have become the minority. The proportion of persons in all socio-professional categories who have gone on to institutions of higher education is growing considerably. These cases have now become the majority for men in the 'employees and sales personnel group'. In addition, it is more common for women in this group as well.

The category 'business, white-collar workers' and intellectual, technical and related professions, can hardly fail to be increasingly restricted to persons having completed university studies in a society where such studies are commonplace. This is precisely what has happened in the United States, according to the data we are now examining.

In the other direction, that of the distribution of members of each formal level of education by socio-professional category, it is the negative aspect of the changes which appear, though with certain nuances (Table 45).

The probability of being a member of the intellectual and related professions has dropped, for all formal levels of instruction, with one minor exception. The decrease is especially striking in the case of university graduates. But - and this is one of the nuances to be noted - these individuals have a greater chance than in the past of belonging to the category 'business, white-collar workers'. The proportion of those who fall into the generally more modest category of employees and sales persons is on the increase.

Overall, the socio-professional level attained after short-term university studies is, likewise, on the decrease. The same can be said for the two following levels of formal of education.

*   *   *

The question arises as to whether the 'increases' and 'decreases' which we have just discussed should be taken literally.

Chapter III suggests that the elevation of formal levels of education is not a reliable indication of the evolution of real levels of culture and of genuine skills. Ad hoc observations would be necessary on this point.

Moreover, given the changes in the nature of curricula corresponding to each formal level of education, like that of the actual situations grouped within each socio-professional category, detailed analyses would also be desirable.

More and more students in higher education are enrolled in programmes whose objectives are quite remote from those of traditional colleges. Even if few of these students, upon completion of their studies, embark upon careers in scientific fields or the liberal professions or obtain positions involving considerable economic or administrative responsibilities, tending to go instead into careers in areas more closely related to their field of study, there is no reason to infer that the level of post-university career opportunities is falling. This is a normal consequence of the evolution of the function of the university. Similarly, the significance of secondary school certificates changes when they cease being the crowning achievement of what was once considered a rather advanced level of schooling, to being regarded as the humble lot of those less adapted to study or of the less motivated.

Imposed characteristics and career

This is the vast realm of 'between-generation' social mobility (social status of origin of the family and one's personal situation in adulthood). It is also where we study the specific incidence of for example region, racial discrimination and sex, on career inequality.

Considered in themselves, these problems, as we have said, are not within the scope of this work. They are only relevant insofar as they relate to schooling.

The network of relationships

We will concentrate on the central problem, namely, the relationships between social background, formal level of education and professional situation.

Since 1965, specialists have examined the network of relationships globally.

Formerly, educational sociology went no further than to examine educational inequality arising from social background, with a tendency to postulate that the selection made by the education system and job allocation were one and the same thing. This led to assertions of the type 'the die is cast' with regard to the professional and social prospects of individuals as soon as the first separation of pupils into streams occurred. This also led to the belief that educational restructuring and the reform of teaching methods as the means of attenuating the inequality of educational opportunity (relationship between social background and qualification) could considerably reduce the inequality of social opportunity (relationship between social background and personal status).

The study of social mobility, meanwhile, confined itself initially to examining the relationship social background/personal situation.

The combination of these two kinds of research revived the problem of the influence of education on social mobility.

Analyses of the network of relationships has, in particular, definitively done away with belief in the strict dependence between the level of one's personal status and formal level of education. The two-way tables (of the type shown in the preceding section) associating these two characteristics already tended to disprove this point of view. An analysis of the network has made even clearer how unrealistic this belief was.

One can, however, debate the extent to which this signifies that the educational selection process has a generally small impact, or a more considerable impact on careers, but allowing for a great degree of variability in the spectrum of situations to which a given type of qualification will lead, depending on the contemporary context.

Let us take a look at these two points of view.

*   *   *

The first hypothesis (educational selection has a lesser influence) is based on multivariate analyses rather similar to those in Chapter IV. The only difference is that the dependent variable - the one at the end of the chain - is the classification of individuals by type of occupation. It is this classification we would like to concentrate on, whereas in Chapter IV, it was the real level of knowledge. The reader can refer to Chapter II on this subject.

Three sorts of fundamental correlations become apparent:

1. Social background of the parents/formal level of education (inequality of educational opportunity).

2. Formal level of education/type of occupation (educational selection and socio-professional breakdown).

3. Social background of the parents/type of occupation (social mobility).

Other correlations are added to these three, depending on the number of variables covered by the analysis: age (and, hence, generation), sex, income (of the parents of those surveyed), test results, attitudes. Some models include ten or more correlations (Sewell & Hauser, 1975).

* * *

Analyses enabling the comparison of both men and women are scarce. Most of them only concern men (Portocarero, 1987).

Figure 12 presents data derived from one of the studies which constitutes an exception. These data relate to the direct explanatory impact (see Chapter IV et seq. on how this differs from the net explanatory impact)of two aspects of social background (taken together) and of the formal level of education on socio-professional category at career start.

The arrow C/IP→D translates the impact of social background on schooling. The formal level of education in this case is explained to the extent of 14% by social background. The weight of the influences which are independent of the latter (around 86%) is six times greater.

The difference according to sex is small. The impact of schooling on individual socio-professional level is markedly more significant. It is greater for women than for men.

Figure 12. France. Men and women. Direct explanatory impacts[1]

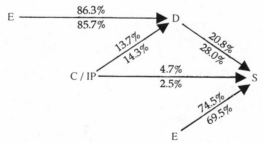

1. C/IP = cumulative direct impact of the father's socio-professional category (C) and his formal level of education (IP). Twenty-seven socio-professional categories, eight formal levels of education. D = formal level of education of the person questioned (eight levels); S = Socio-professional of the persons questioned at the beginning of their careers (twenty seven categories); E = other influences, lumped together. Below the arrows: men; above: women. Data involving the 16 to 52-year old active population at the time of the survey (1972). Tachibanaki, F., *Mobilité sociale et formation en France*. Annales de l'INSEE, No. 28, 1977, p. 129-143, Institut national de la statistique et des études économiques, Paris.

Figure 13. United Kingdom. Men. Net explanatory impacts[1]

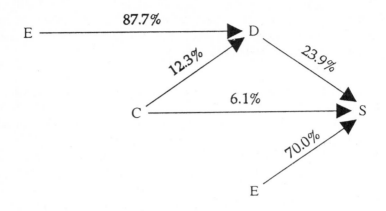

1. C = father's socio-professional category, detailed classification; D = formal level of education of the person questioned (five levels); S = socio-professional classification as for the fathers. Those questioned represent all men aged 20-64 years. England and Wales. Halsey (1978).

The direct impact of social background (C/IP→S) is very small. Ultimately, for both sexes, the main role is played by factors independent of social background and formal level of education (E→S). A more common type of example is given in Figure 13.

The two examples (France, United Kingdom) present a similar pattern of influences. The pattern is typical in its broader aspects to what has been revealed elsewhere in other analyses. The socio-professional classification of individuals, according to this, proves to be extremely uncertain in relation to formal level of education.

This can be observed more simply, as already shown, using two-way tables which indicate the real frequency of types of cases.

* * *

The other hypothesis (significant effects, but variables of the individual formal level of education) does not contradict these realities. It interprets them on the basis of the idea of a queue. When several candidates compete for the same post, it will most likely be awarded to the candidate with the best qualification. This does not mean that the post requires this particular qualification. For instance, it could be that the post is a middle-level position with the customs service and that it is given to a university graduate simply because jobs for graduates are scarce and there are many candidates. Conversely, the post may go to a candidate who merely possesses an elementary school-leaving certificate, being at the top of the list because the other candidates had no qualification at all.

The other characteristics of the candidates also have an impact. It can be supposed that the better the employer - boss or department head - knows the candidates - in particular, having seen them perform - the less importance he will attribute to the qualifications alone. However, in large enterprises and in the civil service, the employer tends to protect himself by justifying his choice only by reference to qualifications. This gives his decision a more impersonal character and avoids embarrassing discussions. When the candidates are unknown, their qualifications are one of the most common means of gaining an appreciation of their abilities. This does not necessarily mean that their educational background corresponds to the qualifications demanded for the post to be filled. A degree in mathematics in itself is not the best qualification for finding employment in an advertising department, but it does make it possible to assume that the candidate is reasonably capable of sustained effort, that he is methodical and that he knows how to obey rules. All that need be done is to bring him up to date.

Extending these common-sense considerations, Raymond Boudon (1979) constructed a mathematical model and made simulations through calculations.

The main working hypothesis is that on the labour market around three-quarters of the highest posts will go to holders of the highest degrees. The remaining posts at this level will be filled according to other, analogous sorting standards, first by holders of qualifications of the second category, then of the third category, etc. These kinds of standards will also apply to the distribution of posts at the other levels.

The model shows that the results obtained on the basis of the overall population, from the point of view of the relationship of schooling to status and from the point of view of social mobility (origin versus status), bears a close resemblance to the actual situation made evident by the surveys and dealt with in multivariate analyses.

This model also shows that the relationship schooling/status and the rate of social mobility, rather than changing when any single parameter, for example, an improvement of the overall formal level of education, changes, evolve as all parameters as a whole change: distribution of families according to social class, distribution of individuals according to formal levels of education, the range of available posts on the labour market, degree of inequality of educational opportunity, etc.

The model shows that, depending on the state of the overall system, a higher general formal level of education and democratization of schooling can nonetheless go hand-in-hand with a decline in the level of the kinds of employment to which various or the majority of qualifications give access, with no improvement in social mobility.

This is what occurs in reality. We have seen this in the case of the relationship qualification/jobs. Meanwhile:

1. The rate of social mobility differs only slightly among industrialized countries, whereas their education systems, on paper at least, are far from uniform (refer to educational policy in the United States, France, Sweden, etc.).

2. The rate of social mobility has barely changed in the past century in these countries, despite the great expansion and democratization of education that has been experienced.

It is not entirely impossible that, theoretically, the composite evolution of social stratification (distribution of families according to standard of living and lifestyle), of the education system (distribution of individuals according to formal level of education, relationship of background to schooling) and of the labour market (spectrum of posts available) can someday produce an increase in social mobility and an increase in outlets for certain categories of qualification.

The evolution of other parameters would also need to be taken into consideration, in particular, that of the relationship formal level of education/real level of skills, that of the rules and practices applying to the granting of posts, and that of the relationships between social background, training (real and formal) and professional aspirations.

*   *   *

The two preceding hypotheses do not contradict each other. They are complementary.

They apply to the same real situation, that is, the 'given' which is to be described and, as far as possible, explained. The second hypotheses refines the explanation.

The two coincide with regard to the role of the educational selection process in the distribution of jobs. Because they represent more than meaningless talk, they cannot, in connection with this point as with any others, limit themselves to the results of observation, which in any case agrees with what both reason and actual experience suggest, namely that the distribution of qualifications and the distribution of jobs do not coincide. They are only partially linked, to a lesser or to a greater extent depending on the country and the type of classification. The first does not govern the second. This is especially evident in connection with the 'queuing' phenomenon. The impact of this phenomenon is most probably considerable, in addition to the influence of actual skills, the successfulness and unsuccessfulness of self-employed individuals, promotion based on seniority, favouritism, discrimination, etc.

In any case, the nature and level of the qualifications only partly condition the nature and level of the job.

Social mobility is again another entity, and is not mechanically linked to either the educational selection process considered alone, or to the distribution of jobs, also considered in isolation. Educational selection, job distribution and social mobility are facets of one system. Each of the types of relationship is dependent on the overall condition of the system of which they are part.

Conclusions

Analysis of the factors related to the distribution of qualifications and of jobs is interesting, although still quite imperfect. It tells us much about the real situation. But these results are approximate and constantly being called into question as further research is conducted.

These efforts should not make us lose sight of the fact that what is most important in practice is the value each factor, not the way in which they are distributed:

1. The qualifications themselves (including the lack of a qualification) as certificates having some influence on professional opportunities and on social status (role of the formal aspect of educational level).

2. The real supplement of knowledge, including professional qualifications, which schooling is to provide, in addition to the contribution it should make in terms of the psychological (equilibrium, dynamism, etc.) and moral (values guiding judgement and conduct) development of the personality.

3. Professional and social status.

A number of factors are involved in the distribution of these factors. Besides sex and 'colour', for example, social background is on of them. According to the available data, its influence on schooling is less significant than that which common belief ascribes to it.

Generally speaking, though the influence of the formal level of education on the kind of position is still greater than that of social background, it is much lower than is commonly believed.

As far as social mobility is concerned (influence of social background on status), it is extremely independent both of educational selection and of the schooling/job relationship.

As concerns social policy, of which educational policy is a facet, the main task is to improve the quality of factors, beginning with a reduction in the extent of the most disadvantaged segments of the population.

From the point of view of qualifications, the worst off are those who do not obtain any qualification at all, or only one of modest value. Because of this, the credentials they can submit to employers are slim, even though their skills may be considerable.

With regard to the distribution of qualifications, reforms concerning the organization of education - including initial training, vocational training, in-service training and continuing education - can accomplish a great deal.

Concerning an improvement in the real level of knowledge and staff development, the task is great and infinitely more difficult. Chapters II and III, limited to the simplest aspects of the problem, provide indications on this subject.

The improvement of status, meanwhile, is a function primarily of economic and social development, more specifically: the effect of income on living conditions, on poverty; its effect on the content of tasks; the sharing of responsibilities in work units; its effect on discrimination as well.

Questions about the most reasonable and the fairest mode of distributing these factors have several facets. At the level of schooling, the main consideration is to avoid failures. To ensure that, independent of the branches into which students are sooner or later channelled, directly or indirectly as a function of the needs of the economy, the real level of education for each person is as elevated as possible, regardless of the social background and other traits. In addition, it is equally important that personal attitudes and characteristics favour, as much as possible, versatility and professional mobility.

These two objectives should satisfy both the demands of personal development and those contributing to the development of society.

It is not utopian to hope for greater dissociation between education as a personal good and professional training in the future. The percentage of literates - to use this somewhat archaic expression - would increase in all classes of society. Insofar as the levels of education thus attained are certified by qualification, the exchange value of these qualifications in the labour market would decline as they become more commonplace. This should not be regarded as a bad thing. There is no reason why 'a worker, a sales girl be less capable of appreciating a play by Shakespeare or of taking the floor in a political meeting than a doctor or an office manager' (Girod, 1981).

The ideal is certainly not each man to his fate according to his qualifications, for life.

As Claparède wrote (1921), each stage of existence - infancy, adolescence and the phases which follow - must be lived to the utmost for itself. Each engenders foci of interest proper to it. Each is rich in possibilities. It is up to education to exploit the development potentialities of little children and, later on, of pupils by considering, as much as possible, each student as an individual case. The individual's subsequent, post-educational, existence will depend on the individual himself/herself and on somewhat unforeseeable circumstances. Normally, the more previous education will have been of benefit, the more adult life, whether professional or extra-professional, should be enhanced. This in no way means that a person's destiny is dictated by schooling.

Just as the democratic objective is to further reduce the dependence between social background and career, it is also just as much to reduce that between qualifications and career, not merely to attenuate that dependence. To strive towards an attenuation of the importance of qualifications would mean a salutary relaxing of the psychological climate during one's school-going years, to increase the margin of individual liberties from a professional point of view, and thereby enabling the economy to adapt with the requisite speed and resilience to changes in technology and the way of life. The opposite, bureaucratic approach, is doomed to paralyzing rigidity. The more ingrained the bureaucratic approach becomes, the more it will produce castes, the crucible of which - woeful prospect - would be the education system.

In this perspective, the results of the observations and analyses mentioned in this chapter, which bring out the fact that the socio-professional level does not depend mechanically on the formal level of education, should be a source of comfort rather than concern.

Bibliography

Adult Performance Level Project (USA), *Adult functional competency: a summary*. Austin, Texas; The University of Texas at Austin, 1975

Andorka, R.; Kolosi, T., *Stratification and inequality*, Budapest, Institute for Social Sciences, 1984

Andorka, R.; Zagórski, K., *Socio-occupational mobility in Hungary and Poland: comparative analysis of surveys, 1972-1973*, Budapest, Central Statistical Office; Warsaw, Central Statistical Office, 1980

Applebee, A. N., et al, *Writing: trends across the decade, 1974-84*, Princeton, NJ; Educational Testing Service, National Assessment of Educational Progress, 1986

Asher, H. B., *Causal modeling*, Beverly Hills, CA; Sage, 1976

Bakker, B. F. M.; Dronkers, J.; Ganzeboom, H. B. G., eds, *Social stratification and mobility in the Netherlands*, Amsterdam; SISWO Publications, 1984

Baudelot, C.; Establet, R., 'Le niveau intellectuel des jeunes conscrits ne cesse de s'élever', *Economie et statistique*, Paris, n° 207, février 1988, 31-39

Baudelot, C.; Establet, R., *Le niveau monte*, Paris; Editions du Seuil, 1989

Bendix, R.; Lipset, S. M., eds, *Class, status and power: a reader in social stratification*, Rev. ed. New York; The Free Press, 1966

Bénéton, P., *Le fléau du bien: essai sur les politiques sociales occidentales (1960-1980)*, Paris; Laffont, 1983

Bernstein, B., *Class, codes and control*, New York; Routledge and Kegan Paul, 1971, 1973 (2 vols)

Bisseret, N., *Les inégaux ou la sélection universitaire*, Paris; Presses universitaires de France, 1974

Blalock, H. M., *Social statistics*, 2nd ed, New York; McGraw-Hill, 1972

Blau, P. M.; Duncan, O. D., *The American occupational structure*, New York; Wiley, 1967.

Bloom, B. S., *Human characteristics and school learning*, New York; McGraw-Hill, 1976

Bornshier, V., 'Social stratification in six Western countries: the general pattern and some differences', *Social science information*, Paris, vol 25, no 4, 1986, 797-824

Boudon, R., *L'analyse mathématique des faits sociaux*, Paris; Librairie Plon, 1967

Boudon, R., *Education, opportunity and social inequality: changing prospects in Western society*, New York; Wiley, 1974

Boudon, R., *Effets pervers et ordre social*, Paris; Presses universitaires de France, 1977

Boudon, R., *L'inégalité des chances: la mobilité sociale dans les sociétés industrielles*, 2nd ed, Paris; Colin, 1979 [first ed 1973]

Boudon, R., *La logique du social: introduction à l'analyse sociologique*, Paris; Hachette, 1979

Boudon, R., *Les mathématiques en sociologie*, Paris; Presses universitaires de France, 1971

Boudon, R.; Bourricaud, F., *Dictionnaire critique de la sociologie*, Paris, Presses universitaires de France, 1982

Bourdieu, P.; Passeron, J.-C., *The inheritors: French students and their relation to culture. With a new epilogue, 1979*, Chicago; University of Chicago Press, 1979

Bourdieu, P.; Passeron, J.-C., *Reproduction in education, society and culture*, London; Sage, 1977

Bovet, P., *Les examens de recrues dans l'armée suisse, 1854-1913*, Newchâtel, Switzerland; Delachaux & Niestlé, 1935

Bowles, S.; Glatis, H., *Schooling in capitalist America: educational reform and the contradictions of economic life*, New York; Basic Books, 1976

Boyd, M., et al, *Ascription and achievement: studies in mobility and status attainment in Canada*, Ottawa; Carleton University Press, 1985

Brown, R.; Bowditch, D., *Adult readers: will they need basics too?* Denver, CO; national Assessment of Educational Progress, Education Commission of the States, 1979

Buros, O. K., ed, *The seventh mental measurements yearbook*, Highland Park, NJ; The Gryphon Press, 1972

Caplow, T., *The sociology of work*, New York; McGraw-Hill, 1964

Carnoy, M.; Levin, H. M., *The limits of educational reform*, New York; Longman, 1978

Cherkaoui, M., *Les changements du système éducatif en France, 1950-1980*, Paris, Presses universitaires de France, 1972

Cherkaoui, M., *Les paradoxes de la réussite scolaire: sociologie comparée des systèmes d'enseignement*, Paris, Presses universitaires de France, 1979

Cherkaoui, M., *Sociologie de l'éducation*, Paris, Presses universitaires de France, 1986

Claparède, E., *L'éducation fonctionelle*, 7th ed, Neuchâtel, Switzerland; Delachaux & Niestlé, 1964 (1st ed 1921)

Clark, B., *Educating the expert society*, San Francisco; Chandler Publishing Co, 1962

Coleman, J. S., 'The concept of equality of educational opportunity', *Harvard educational review*, Cambridge MA, vol 38, no 1, Winter 1968, 7-22

Coleman, J. S., et al, *Equality of opportunity*, Washington DC; US Office of Education, 1966

Coleman, J. S., 'Methods and results in the IEA studies of effects of school on learning', *Review of educational research*, Washington DC, vol 45, no 3, 355-386

College Board (USA), *Taking the SAT: the official guide to the Scholastic Aptitude Test and Test of Standard Written English*, Rev. ed., Princeton, NJ; Admissions Testing Programs, College Board, 1986

Comber, L. C.; Keeves, J.-P., *Science education in nineteen countries*, New York; Wiley and Stockholm; Almqvist & Wiksell, 1973

The condition of education: statistical report, Washington DC; National Center for Education Statistics, annual

Dahrendorf, R., *Life chances: approaches to social and political theory*, Chicago; University of Chicago Press, 1981

Digest of education statistics, Washington DC; National Center for Education Statistics, annual

Dobzhansky, T., *Genetic diversity and human equality: the facts and fallacies in the explosive genetics and education controversy*, New York; Basic Books, 1973

Données sociales, Paris; Institut national de la statistique et des études économiques 1973-1987, 6 vols

Dronkers, J.; Jong, U. de, 'Jencks and Fägerlind in a Dutch way: a report on research on the relationship between social background, intelligence, education, occupation and income in the Netherlands', *Social science information/Information sur les sciences sociales*, Paris, vol 18, nos 4-5, 1979, 761-781

Duncan, O. D.; Featherman, D. L.; Duncan, B., *Socioeconomic background and achievement*, New York; Seminar Press, 1972

Faure, E., et al, *Learning to be: the world of education today and tomorrow*, Paris; Unesco and London; Harrap, 1972

Fitouri, C.; 'Biculturalism, bilingualism and scholastic achievement in Tunisia', *Prospects*, Paris; Unesco, vol XIV, no 1, 1984, 75-85

Fitouri, C.; 'Biculturalisme, bilingualisme et réussite scolaire en Tunisie', *Perspectives*, Paris; Unesco, vol XIX, no 1, 1984, 77-88

Gendre, F., *L'analyse statistique multivariée*, Geneva; Librairie Droz, 1976

Girod, R., *Politiques de l'éducation: l'illusoire et le possible*, Paris, Presses universitaires de France, 1981

Girod, R., et al, *L'éventail des connaissances: niveau des recrues dans quelques domaines*, Aarau, Switzerland; Sauerländer, 1987. Examens pédagogiques des recrues: série scientifique, vol IX

Girod, R., *Les inégalités sociales*, Paris, Presses universitaires de France, 1984

Goldthorpe, J. H.; Llewellyn, C.; Payne, C., *Social mobility and class structure in modern Britain*, Oxford; Clarendon Press, 1980

Gruber, E. C.; Bramson, M., *Scholastic Aptitude Test (SAT) for college entrance*, New York; Simon & Schuster, 1983

Gruson, P.; Markiewicz-Lagneau, J., *L'énseignement supérieur et son efficacité: France, Etats-Unis, URSS, Pologne*, Paris; La Documentation française, 1983

Hallack, J., *A qui profite l'école?*, Paris, Presses universitaires de France, 1974

Halsey, A. H., ed, *Ability and educational opportunity*, Paris; OECD, 1961

Halsey, A. H.; Floud, J.; Anderson, C. A., eds, *Education, economy and society: a reader in the sociology of education*, New York; The Free Press of Glencoe, 1961

Halsey, A. H.; Heath, A. F.; Ridge, J. M., *Origins and destinations: family, class and education in modern Britain*, Oxford; Clarendon Press, 1980

Havighurst, R. J.; Neugarten, B. L., *Society and education*, 2nd ed, Boston MA; Allyn & Bacon, 1962

Holmes, B. J.; Wright, D., *What do young adults know about science? Some results from two National Assessments*, Denver, CO; Assessment of Educational Progress, Education Commission of the States, 1980

Hueftle, S. J.; Rakow, S. J.; Welch, W. W., *Images of science: a summary of results from the 1981-1982 national assessment in science*, Minneapolis, MN; University of Minnesota, Minnesota Research and Evaluation Center, 1983

Hummel, C., *Education today for the world of tomorrow*, Paris; Unesco, 1977

Hurn, C. J., *The limits and possibilities of schooling: an introduction to the sociology of education*, Boston, MA; Allyn & Bacon, 1978

Husén, T., ed, *International study of achievement in mathematics: a comparison of twelve countries*, Stockholm; Almqvist & Wiksell and New York; Wiley, 1967 (2 vols)

Husén, T., *Social background and educational career: research perspectives on equality of educational opportunity*, Paris; OECD, CERI, 1972

Husén, T., 'Policy implications of individual differences in learning ability: a comparative perspective', *Scandinavian journal of educational research*, Oslo, vol 22, no 4, 1978, 173-191

Husén, T., *The school in question: a comparative study of the school and its future in Western society*, Oxford; Oxford University Press, 1979

Husén, T., *Talent, equality and meritocracy: availability and utilization of talent*, The Hague; Martinus Nijhoff, 1974 (Plan Europe 2000, Project 1, vol 9)

Husén, T.; Postlethwaite, T. N., eds, *The international encyclopedia of education*, Oxford; Pergamon Press, 1985 (10 vols)

Institut national d'études démographiques (France): Institut national d'étude du travail et d'orientation professionnelle, (France), *Enquête nationale sur le niveau intellectuel des enfants d'âge scolaire*, Paris; Presses universitaires de France, 1969, 1973, 1978 (INED. Travaux et documents. Cahiers, nos 54, 64 and 83)

Institut national d'études démographiques (France), *'Population' et l'enseignement. Recueils d'études dur l'éducation parus dans la revue Population de 1960 à 1969*, Paris, Presses universitaires de France, 1970 (English edition published 1972)

Jencks, C., et al, *Inequality: a reassessment of the effect of family and schooling in America*, New York; Basic Books, 1972

Jencks, C., et al, *Who gets ahead? The determinants of economic success in America*, New York; Basic Books, 1979

Jensen, A. R., *Educability and group differences*, New York; Harper & Row, 1973

Kaelbel, H., *Social mobility in the 19th and 20th centuries: Europe and America in comparative perspective*, New York; St Martin's Press, 1986

Karabel, J.; Halsey, A. H., eds, *Power and ideology in education: a reader*, New York; Oxford University Press, 1977

Kirsch, I. S.; Jungeblat, A., *Literacy: profiles of America's young adults. Final report*, Princeton, NJ; National Assessment of Educational Progress, Educational Testing Service, 1986

Levine, D. M.; Bane, M. J., eds, *The 'inequality' controversy: schooling and distributive justice*, New York; Basic Books, 1975

Lipset, S. M.; Bendix, R., *Social mobility and social structure*, London, Routledge and Kegan Paul, 1986 (1st edition 1959)

Lyons-Morris, L.; Fitz-Gibbon, C. T., *How to measure achievement: program evaluation kit*, Beverly Hills, CA; Sage, 1978

Mach, B.; Wesolowski, W., *Social mobility and social structure*, London; Routledge and Kegan Paul, 1986

McKnight, C. C., et al, *The underachieving curriculum: assessing US school mathematics from an international perspective*, Second Mathematical Study, Champaign, IL; Stipes, 1987

Mosteller, F.; Moynihan, D. P., eds, *On equality of educational opportunity: papers deriving from the Harvard University Faculty Seminar on the Coleman Report*, New York; Random House, 1972

Müller, W., *Familie, Schule, Beruf: Analysen zur sozialen Mobilität und Statuszuweizung in der Bundesrepublik*, Opladen, FRG; Westdeutscher Verlag, 1975

Müller, W.; Mayer, U. K., eds, *Social stratification and career mobility*, Paris; Mouton, 1973

Mullis, I. V. S.; Oldefendt, S. J.; Phillips, D. L., *What students know and can do: profiles of three age groups*, Denver, CO; National Assessment of Educational Progress, Education Commission of the States, 1977

National Assessment of Educational Progress (USA), *Three national assessments of science: changes in achievement, 1969-1977*, Denver, CO; National Assessment of Educational Progress, Education Commission of the States, 1978

National Assessment of Educational Progress (USA), *The third national mathematics assessment: results, trends and issues*, Denver, CO; National Assessment of Educational Progress, Education Commission of the States, 1983

National Assessment of Educational Progress (USA), *Three National Assessments of reading: changes in performance, 1970-1980*, Denver, CO; National Assessment of Educational Progress, Education Commission of the States, 1981

National Assessment of Educational Progress (USA), *The reading report card: progress toward excellence in our schools. Trends in reading over four national assessments, 1971-1984*, Princeton, NJ; National Assessment of Educational Progress, Educational Testing Service, 1985

National Assessment of Educational Progress (USA), *A nation at risk: the imperative for educational reform. A report to the Nation and the Secretary of Education, Department of Education*, by the National Commission on Excellence in Education. Chairman: D. P. Gardner. Washington DC; Superintendent of Documents, US Government Printing Office, 1983

Nie, N. H., et al, *Statistical package for the social sciences (SPSS)*, 2nd ed, New York; McGraw-Hill, 1975

OECD, *Education, inequality and life chances/L'éducation, les inégalités et les chances de la vie*, Paris, 1975 (2 vols)

Parsons, T., *Essays in sociological theory*, rev. ed., New York; The Free Press, 1962 (1st ed 1954)

Parsons, T., *Social structure and personality*, New York; The Free Press, 1964

Parsons, T., *The social system*, New York; The Free Press, 1965 (1st ed 1951)

Parsons, T., *Structure and process in modern societies*, New York; The Free Press, 1960

Parsons, T., et al, *Family, socialization and interaction process*, New York; The Free Press, 1955

Parsons, T., et al, *Theories of society*, New York; The Free Press, 1965 (2 vols)

Passow, A. H., et al, *The National Case Study: an empirical comparative study if twenty-one educational systems*, Stockholm; Almqvist & Wiksell and New York; Wiley, 1976 (International studies in evaluation, VII)

Peaker, G. F., *An empirical study of education in twenty one countries: a technical report*, Stockholm; Almqvist & Wiksell and New York; Wiley, 1975 (International studies in evaluation, VIII)

Persell, C. H., *Education and inequality*, New York; The Free Press, 1977

Petitat, A., *Production de l'école - production de la societé: analyse sociohistorique de quelques moments décisifs de l'évolution scolaire en Occident*, Geneva; Librairie Droz, 1982

Piaget, J., *Biologie et connaissance*, 3rd ed, Paris; Gallimard, 1973 (1st ed 1967)

Pöntinen, S., *Social mobility and social structure: a comparison of Scandinavian countries*, Helsinki; The Finnish Society of Sciences and Letters, 1983

Pöntinen, S.; Uusitalo, H., 'Socioeconomic background and income', *Acta sociologica*, Copenhagen, vol 18, no 4, 1975, 322-329

Portocarero, L., *Social mobility in industrial societies: women in France and Sweden*, Stockholm; Almqvist & Wiksell for the Swedish Institute for Social Research, 1987

Prost, A., *L'enseignement s'est-il démocratise?*, Paris, Presses universitaires de France, 1986

Purves, A. C.; Levine, D. U., eds, *Educational policy and international assessment: implications of the IEA surveys of achievement*, Berkeley, CA; McCutchan, 1975

Robin, D.; Barrier, E., *Enquête internationale sur l'enseignement des mathématiques*, Tome 1, *Les cas français*, Paris, Institut national de recherche pédagogique, 1985

Sauvy, A., *L'économie du diable: chômage et inflation*, Paris; Calmann-Lévy, 1976

Sauvy, A.; Girard, A., 'Les diverses classes sociales devant l'enseignement', *Population*, Paris, no 2, March-April 1965, 205-232. Reprinted in *'Population' et l'enseignement*, op. cit., 233-260

Sauvy, A.; Girard, A., *Vers l'enseignement pour tous*, Brussells; Elsevier-Séquoia, 1974

Schnaper, D, 'Sélection: le poids des mots', *Commentaire*, Paris, no 37, Spring 1987, 200-204

Sewell, W. H.; Hauser, R. M., *Education, occupation and earnings: achievement in the early career*, New York; Viking Press

Sewell, W. H.; Hauser, R. M.; Featherman, D. L., eds, *Schooling and achievement in American society*, New York; Academic Press, 1975

Sexton, P, *Education and income: inequalities of opportunity in our public schools*, New York; Viking Press, 1964

Siguan, M.; Mackey, W. F., *Education and bilingualism*, London; Kogan Page, 1987

Sorokin, P. A., *Comment la civilisation se transforme*, Paris; Librairie Marcel Rièvre, 1964 (translation of a fundamental chapter in *Social and cultural dynamics*)

Sorokin, P. A., *Social and cultural dynamics: a study of change in major systems of art, truth, ethics, law and social relationships*, rev and abridged ed, Boston MA; Sargent, 1957 (1st ed published in 4 vols between 1937 and 1941)

Sorokin, P. A., *Social and cultural mobility*, enl ed, New York; The Free Press, 1964 (1st ed 1927)

Sorokin, P. A., *Society, culture and personality: their structure and dynamics. A system of general sociology*, New York; Cooper Square Publishers, 1962 (1st ed 1947)

Steedman, L. C.; Kaestle, C. F., *An investigation of crude literacy, reading performance and functional literacy in the United States, 1880 to 1980*, Madison WI; Wisconsin Center for Education Research, University of Wisconsin, 1986

Suisse, Département fédéral de l'intérieur. Bureau de statistique, *Examen pédagogique des recrues*, Berne, 1876-1914

Tanguy, L., ed, *L'introuvable relation formation/emploi*, Paris; la Documentation française, 1986

Thélot, C., *Tel père, tel fils? Position sociale et origine familiale*, Paris; Dunod, 1982

Thorndike, R. L., *Reading comprehension education in fifteen countries:an empirical study*, International studies in evaluation III, New York; Wiley and Stockholm; Almqvist & Wiksell, 1973

Treiman, D. J., *Occupational prestige in comparative perspective*, New York; Academic Press, 1977

Unesco, Office of Statistics, Division of Statistics on Education, *Statistics of educational attainment and illiteracy/Statistiques sur le niveau de l'instruction et de l'analphabétisme*, Paris, 1983

USA, Department of Commerce, Bureau of the Census, *Social indicators 1976*, Washington DC, Superintendent of Documents; US Government Printing Office, 1977

Van de Geer, J. P., *Introduction to multivariate analysis for the social sciences*, San Francisco; Freeman, 1971

Vimont, C., *L'avenir de l'emploi: l'illusoire, le possible. Réflexions sur les mécanismes de l'emploi et du chômage*, Paris; Economica, 1981

Walker, D. A., *The IEA six subject survey: an empirical study of education in twenty-one countries* (International studies in evaluation, IX), Stockholm; Almqvist & Wiksell International and New York; Wiley, 1976

Warner, W. L.; Havighurst, R. J.; Loeb, M. B., *Who shall be educated?*, New York; Harper, 1944

Weiss, P., *La mobilité sociale*, Paris, Presses universitaires de France, 1986

Wesolowski, W.,; Slomczynski, K.; Mach, B., eds, *Social mobility in comparative perspective*, Warsaw, Ossolineum, 1978

Wright, D., et al, *Three assessments of science, 1969-1977: technical summary*, Denver CO; National Assessment of Educational Progress, Education Commission of the States, 1979

Wright, S. R. *Quantitative methods and statistics: a guide to social research*, Beverly Hills CA; Sage, 1979

Yoskum, C. S.; Yerkes, R. M., *Army mental tests*, New York; Holt, 1920

Young, M., *The rise of meritocracy, 1870-2033: an essay in education and equality*, London; Thames and Hudson, 1961 (1st ed 1958)